THE
BIBLE
CAN
CHANGE
YOU

THE BIBLE CAN CHANGE YOU

How the Word of God Heals Your Life

MARILYN HICKEY

Creation House
Lake Mary, Florida

Creation House
Strang Communications Company
600 Rinehart Road
Lake Mary, FL 32746

Unless otherwise noted, all Scripture quotations are from the Holy Bible, New International Version. Copyright © 1973, 1978, 1984, International Bible Society. Used by permission. Scripture quotations marked KJV are from the King James Version.

First Printing, November 1989
Second Printing, May 1990

Dedication

*To my husband, Wally, my daughter, Sarah,
and my mother, Mary, who have always been
encouraging and supportive, not only in the best
of times but also in discouraging times. They
have reminded me to teach the
Word and to live it.*

Contents

 O N E

When the Word of God Comes to You   9

T W O

Hagar: Hope for the Hopeless   21

T H R E E

Esther: Fire That Doesn't Burn   33

F O U R

Eli: Meeting the God Who Loves   49

F I V E

Elijah: Shining for God—or Burning Out?   65

S I X

Habakkuk: Answers From God's Silence   83

S E V E N

Ruth: Part of the Curse or Part of the Blessing   101

E I G H T

Ezra: Make Up Your *Heart* About God   121

N I N E

Deborah: Just Do It!   139

ONE

When the Word of God Comes to You

E very time I open the leather cover of my Bible, I have a sense of wonder. Here in my hands is a treasure chest of wisdom, guidance, counsel, principles for practical, successful living and spiritual food.

I love the Bible, because it's the word of God!

But so often, when I'm reading, I recall the times I've been confused about what I should do in a real-life situation. And I think of the many cries and complaints I've heard through the years I've been in public ministry, heartfelt pleas from men and women searching for some solid word from God to direct or to stabilize their lives:

"If God had warned me—shouted in my ear or sent someone to stop me—I'd never have gotten into this mess."

"I wish the Bible were more specific on situations like...."

"I'm not one of these people who 'hears' God's voice all the time. Why does it have to be so hard to know what God wants to say to me?"

"I've gone to five different Christians for advice and counsel, and every one of them told me something different. So how am I supposed to know what to do?"

"I'd love it if God would just say yes or no when I ask Him about certain things. But He doesn't speak to me that clearly."

"Yeah, the Bible's great. But I'm not sure how to connect with it. If only God would talk to me in plain English."

There are two issues at stake here. One is our constant need to know how to handle real, everyday challenges. You and I need to know how to understand God's word to us.

And if God's voice is not clear-cut to you, relax! He wants to change that.

Your need for specific direction in everyday matters is of great concern to God. Questions such as what job to take, whom to marry, where to go to school, what to do about a problem with your friend—these things are important to us. They're important to Him, too. And God isn't bothered one bit if we come to Him with the most trivial matter or one that's earthshaking. As James says, "If any of you lacks wisdom, he should ask God, who gives generously to all without finding fault" (James 1:5).

God wants to give us wisdom. He always wants to speak to us. So I look at it this way: If I lack wisdom on how to handle a certain situation, then the problem is quite likely with my inability to *hear* Him or how His word applies to me.

I must admit that I often wish God's personal word to me would show up in big, bold letters across the sky. Maybe King Belshazzar didn't like God's handwriting on the wall, but at least the message came across loud and clear: "I've weighed you in My balance, Belshazzar. And you've been found pitifully lacking." That powerful, Babylonian tyrant had no question about God's warning: "Humble yourself in dust and sackcloth and repent of the satanic pride that makes you think you're a god!" (See Dan. 5.)

Many of us, though, myself included, are often stumped as to what God's thinking. You pray. Then you get up off your knees, and it's like standing up in a fog. Nothing's clear! ◐

Let's say, for example, that Christian parents find their teenage son (the one who used to win honors pins in Sunday school for knowing all the memory verses) is now taking drugs.

Immediately, they're faced with a whole bunch of choices and questions: Do they take a "tough love" approach and throw him out of the house until he quits, or do they pour on unconditional love? Do they call in the youth pastor who used to do drugs, or check the boy into a rehab center? Do they search their hearts for times past when they wounded their son emotionally, then seek his forgiveness? Or do they determine that Satan has broken through their ranks, and begin to do spiritual warfare on behalf of their boy? Or is it all of the above?

I don't know about you, but I've heard countless testimonies about kids who were rescued from drugs. It seems as if no two were alike. One couple used "tough love"; another poured on unconditional love. One broke the bondage through prayer; another, through repentance. And each time, the mom or dad said, "The Holy Spirit told us what to do, and we did it."

Do you see my point? God's word in the Bible doesn't have a one-answer-fits-all section when it comes to many of our specific needs.

Obviously, knowing God's thoughts on a given matter requires that we walk closely with Him every day. It means staying in touch with Him by reading His word, praying and having fellowship with brothers and sisters in Christ so we can hear His voice through them, too. These are some of the basics for anyone to grow in faith.

Throughout this book, you'll learn more about these foundational principles—things that will help you when you need counsel, wisdom and advice from the Lord.

But there's another, more intriguing aspect to God's word.

It is thought that Paul wrote the book of Hebrews. Paul had been startled often enough by God's revelation, so he knew exactly what he was talking about when he wrote this: "The word of God is living and active, sharper than any double-edged sword" (Heb. 4:12).

Living and active! Did you know that God's word is more than principles to be applied? Did you know His living word wants to encounter you—meet you face-to-face?

If you feel restless, dissatisfied, wanting something more for your spiritual life, then I've got great news for you! These are all signs that God wants you to meet His living, active word in a new way. He wants to break through deadness, dullness and dryness. He wants to speak a word to you that will settle at the bottom of your soul forever, a foundation stone from which He can call you to come up higher with Him.

God wants your inner man to be energized in a new way—transformed—just as meat and drink become living, healthy tissue to your physical body. God wants not only to change your situation, but He also wants to transform *you.*

Sounds wonderful, doesn't it? And it is!

But, believe me, God's fresh, new word to you isn't always easy to accept. I know—from tough, personal experience.

I was raised in a good, Methodist church that gave me a certain love for the Bible. I loved learning, language and logic, so by the time I was in ninth grade I knew what I wanted to do with my life: study and teach about words and languages. College gave me a teaching certificate, and, by age twenty-three, I launched into the career I'd mapped out for myself in education. I loved my job as a teacher, and I knew what I wanted, thank you.

There was only one big problem. My plan hit a couple of snags.

First, there was my mother. She'd become one of those "spooky" Christians who always talked about the Holy Spirit as if she knew Him. It was unnerving enough to eat dinner at her house and hear all these stories about how God was moving in people's lives. I suspected that, secretly, she was praying for me. This nagging fear kept poking me in the ribs: What if God had something else in mind for me to do with my life?

And then I did the craziest thing.

I started dating a guy named Wally, another one of these Spirit-filled Christian types. Except for the fact that he was sweet and I was attracted to him, I thought I had to be nuts. My idea of a date was dinner, dancing and a movie. His idea of a date was dinner and *church!*

I had an inkling that he had joined together with Mom in praying for me. What was I getting myself into?

Once Wally even had the nerve to show up late, then tell me he was late because he'd been fasting—for me! I was insulted.

Just about that time, I began to have trouble sleeping. Night after night, a vague uneasiness left me staring wide-eyed at the ceiling. Sometimes, just to focus my roller-coaster thoughts, I began to read my Bible into the early morning hours.

Now I was not big on Bible reading at that time, let me assure you. The Bible was a disturbing book in many ways. But reading it was the only thing that brought rest. Even then, I wasn't about to admit that Mom and Wally had found something real that I didn't have. (One night when Mom walked in and surprised me, I stuffed the Bible under my pillow so she wouldn't see me reading it and get too excited.)

On one of those long, sleepless nights, I sensed a strong stirring inside. I recognized the voice of God, speaking clearly in my heart, saying, "You are born of My Spirit, and you're My child, but...."

I knew what the "but" was all about. I had never given God permission to direct my life.

In the pause that followed, I saw—as in a vision—my whole life, passing in a flash. I saw my career in education and the life I'd planned for myself. It looked pretty good.

And then, in my mind's eye, I tried to turn and

glimpse God's plan for me. The vision closed!

"But," the inner voice of the Spirit continued, "I've been dealing with you for some time, and I'm not going to deal with you anymore. You can go your own way if that's what you want."

Laying my head back on the pillow I looked up at that blank ceiling. Here I was—Marilyn, the Practical Planner—and God was asking me to make a choice on blind faith!

I lay there for a long time. God's word had come to me, asking me to choose. This Bible that sat open on the bedclothes had spoken to me. I'd read about men and women whose lives were changed by God. But there was something else.

For the first time, it occurred to me that this book was the most powerful book I'd read. Not only were its printed words a challenge to my mind, but another spiritual power was at work here. The printed word was acting together with another voice. One that was calling me now.

And it was saying, "You believe in My word. Now let it take hold of your life and transform you."

"OK, Lord," I finally prayed. "Whatever You want."

That night I surrendered my life to Christ.

There were lots of bends in the path after that. Wally and I did marry, of course. And it was years before God opened the way to the international teaching ministry He had in His plan for me. But no turning point was quite so important as that night alone in my room when I came face-to-face with God's living word and its transforming power.

Because of that night and the tremendous changes that followed, I've become keenly alert whenever I read a passage, especially in the Old Testament, that begins: "The word of the Lord came to me, saying..." or "The word of the Lord came to so-and-so...." They've made me realize something.

Except for one thin, three-and-a-half-year slice of history when Jesus spoke in a human voice to a few thousand men and women on a narrow strip of land in the Middle East, all the rest of us, before and after, have had to encounter "the word of God" entirely through the Spirit.

In the chapters that follow, I want to introduce you to some men and women from the Old Testament. Some of them are well-known figures. Others, perhaps, you've paid less attention to.

What was it like for men like Eli, Elijah, Habakkuk and Ezra when the word of the Lord came to them? What happened to women like Hagar, Esther, Deborah and Ruth who faced the choice of following God's directive—or their own way? And, more important, how were their lives forever altered by their encounter with the living word?

These are men and women who, like you and me, never bumped into Jesus while drawing water from a well. (Or, I should say, while grocery shopping!) Like us, they faced tremendous personal pressures—the need for courage in the face of international upheavals, people who didn't understand their faith, personal hardship, mental and emotional suffering, marital strife, physical burnout, children who went astray. In no way were they exempt from any of the soul-crushing challenges that can rise against us today.

There's a cautionary side to this. Some, like Eli, missed God's cue. Because they didn't press into God, they allowed evil to overtake them. That doesn't need to be so for any one of us.

But others—Elijah, Esther, Habakkuk, Ruth, Ezra—each one made a different discovery. Long before their awaited Messiah walked the green hills of Israel, they learned that God's word is not only like a sword; it's living water, flowing like a refreshing stream from the throne of God to water and renew the thirst that's in our souls.

What is your situation right now? Do you need a drink of that living word to soothe your dryness and get you recharged? To cleanse and heal mental, emotional or spiritual wounds? To give you solid footing and clear direction?

Whatever you need, your life can be transformed. You can learn from the lives of the men and women of Scripture and from the lives of contemporary brothers and sisters in Christ—each of whom encountered the word of God in a unique way.

I promise you: If you read this book, with not only

an attentive mind but also an open spirit, change is inevitable.

But a word of caution: Proceed only if you're ready to let go of the known and comfortable and step up to new realms of the Spirit. Because the word of God is more than print on pages. It can change your life!

TWO

Hagar: Hope for the Hopeless

How many times have you been tempted to think God has big plans only for "important" people? Maybe it's that we think He cares about leaders more than He cares about everyday, ordinary moms, dads, business people, teachers, secretaries and auto mechanics.

Underneath, even if we don't realize it, we assume that He has more time for these important people, that He'll give more attention to His favored group. When we need Him, though, He'll be too busy.

Now here's the problem with that kind of wrong-headed thinking. From time to time, life pushes each one of us up against a wall. People get fired. Marriages hit the rocks. Children rebel. Health problems hit.

If you think God has time only for the important people—and you're not one of them—I can tell you how you'll feel: overlooked, hopeless!

It's time for you to meet a special "little" person, one who is among the most overlooked people in all of Scripture. Now this lady was facing hopeless circumstances. I'm referring to Hagar, the Egyptian slave-girl who served Sarah.

Hagar had an encounter with the living, active word of God that set her life on a whole new course. Not only that, but because of her response, God placed Hagar at the head of a plan to create a mighty nation (the Arabs) through her son Ishmael. Hagar's story, so often overshadowed by that of Abraham and Sarah, holds crucial principles and revelations for you and me.

Hagar's situation is pretty awful, right from the first moment we meet her. In Genesis 16 we find her in the company of Abraham, the patriarch and father of our faith, and Sarah. But the fact of the matter is, being in their company at all was a huge part of Hagar's problem.

You see, not long after Abraham left Ur and reached the promised land, there was a famine.

Now it's quite likely that God would have performed a miracle and provided for His family supernaturally, just the way He would rain manna from heaven for the Israelites several hundred years later. But Abraham wasn't totally tuned in to God yet. He jumped the gun and hightailed it down to Egypt—a trip of a thousand miles! In doing so, he stepped out of God's will.

Among the other problems Abraham brought upon himself because of this troublesome little side trip was an enormous domestic rift. And who took the brunt of all the guff?

Enter Hagar.

Sarah purchased Hagar to be her personal slave. Who knows what abuse this girl had suffered at the hands of her Egyptian slave-masters? The fact that her name means "flight" may be a clue that, whatever she'd been through, she'd learned one thing—how to run! That was one skill she was going to need.

You see, even though Abraham's household was under the protection of God Himself, serving Sarah was no picnic. Immediately, Hagar was plunged into what you and I would call a no-win situation—one of terrific proportions.

Abraham's household returned to the promised land, and at the end of Genesis 15, we read the bombastic account of God's covenant with Abraham. Abraham sacrificed to God and later, when darkness fell, a blazing torch and smoking fire pot passed between the severed pieces of the sacrificial animals—a heifer, a goat and a ram. God had already promised to make Abraham into a great nation (see Gen. 12:2). Now He promised to give to Abraham's countless descendants the great and beautiful land of Israel on which he stood (see Gen. 15:18-21). When Sarah heard this promise, her eyebrows must have shot up.

As she saw it, God had overlooked one tiny detail: She was barren—not to mention the fact that she was in her early seventies! Where were all these descendants supposed to come from? If Abraham hadn't gotten the idea that the Lord could provide food, Sarah surely hadn't caught on to the fact that it would be no problem for Him to give her a child!

So Sarah did something that many of us are famous for: She decided to help God out a little bit. She offered Hagar to Abraham, saying, "Go, sleep with my maidservant; perhaps I can build a family through her" (see Gen. 16:2). It wasn't long before the girl turned up pregnant.

Now imagine Hagar's viewpoint on this whole business. Here she is, pregnant by Sarah's husband, carrying a child that Sarah wants for her own—and Hagar's still expected to sweep this lady's floors, bake her bread and haul water for her. Things got hot! When Hagar rebelled, Sarah lost it and became abusive to the poor girl.

That's when Hagar did the first thing that came naturally to her. She took flight.

Out of Abraham's encampment she fled into the wilderness of Shur, where she immediately lost her way. Interestingly enough, *Shur* means "wall." Hagar was very much up against the wall!

How many times have you felt like Hagar—in a wilderness, with your back up against a wall, in a bad situation that's not even of your own making?

Did you know that when things are the roughest, that's exactly the moment God wants to speak to you? So often, it seems as if God backs us up against a wall so He can get through to us. Actually, it's more accurate to say that we usually aren't paying attention too closely, until circumstances press in. Then we're all ears!

But there's something in Hagar's story, something in her response, that's most important. Take a close look.

When the angel of the Lord came, bearing God's word to Hagar, he found her pregnant and pitiful. There she sat, by a small spring in the hot, rugged desert. She was physically spent, miserable, despondent.

"Hagar, servant of Sarah," the angel greeted her, "where have you come from, and where are you going?" (Obviously he knew where she'd come from, so I'd guess he was more interested in the second part of the question.)

"I'm running away from my mistress," she responded. Yet she couldn't tell him where she was headed, because she had no idea. Right at that moment, Hagar no doubt felt as if she could use a little sympathy.

You'd almost expect the angel to say, "Oh, you poor,

dear thing. We've been looking down on you from heaven and—boy!—have you had it rough. Keep movin' on, honey. Run as far away from this mess as you can get." But that wasn't the case.

The angel declared God's word to her: "Go back to your mistress and submit to her!" (see Gen. 16:9).

If I were Hagar I'd be shocked, wouldn't you? "What? Go back to that mean, abusive old thing? You've got to be kidding."

But before she could open her mouth long enough to stick her foot in it, the angel did something very beautiful. He gave her a glimpse of God's higher plan—if she would obey it.

He said, "Your descendants through this child will so increase that they'll be too numerous to count." He also told her that she was carrying a son, and that she should name him *Ishmael*, which means "God hears."

Note Hagar's precious response. Remember, she had no promise that Sarah wouldn't continue the abuse. But what did she say? "Not only does God hear; He is the God who sees me, too!"

In other words, she was saying, it's not just that God overheard some stray report that's floating around heaven about my bad circumstances. His eye is on me. He's watching over me, and even in all this He has a plan.

Let me ask you: When God's word comes to you, how do you respond?

Unfortunately, there are a lot of times when we want

to flee. Some people take a bad situation and make it worse. They waste their lives in self-pity and depression. Or they sink themselves into sin—drinking, taking drugs, hopping from one relationship to the other or selling out to materialism. In their hearts they do nothing but blame God.

Maybe, like Hagar, you're in a position you just don't like. Things are definitely not going your way. You hate it! Like Hagar, you want to flee. But then—while praying or reading Scripture or talking to a Christian friend or hearing a preacher on TV—God's word comes to you loud and strong.

You say, "I've got to get out of this rotten marriage. Surely God wants me to be happy and fulfilled. And I'll never be happy as long as I'm married to that so-and-so." But God says, "Stay right where you are. It won't be easy, but I'm a God of miracles and I can restore your marriage."

You say, "My work situation is the pits! It's so bad I can hardly drag myself out of bed in the morning. Those people are pure heathens! They promised me a raise three years ago, and I haven't seen a penny of it. I really resent the way they make me feel used!" But God says, "Love those who hate you and despitefully use you. Do your job as if you were serving Me alone. The ability to promote is in My hands, not theirs."

You say, "How could that child do such a horrible thing and hurt me like this? I'm destroyed! He's a total loss to the human race, let alone to God." But God says, "Get on your knees and pray, and don't get up until you see the full restoration of this beloved one. Because that's My will!"

What do you do when you're against a wall and God's word comes to you? You have to choose, just as I had the choice to continue my career in teaching. He didn't make me to be a puppet. In the same way, you can choose to tune Him out and head in your own direction.

Or you can obey Him. •

Hagar, who was used to running away, chose to obey. She accepted what He said as true. She purposed in her heart not to run again, but to trust Him—to believe that His will for her was only good.

I'm convinced that that gave her the strength to make what was probably the most difficult move she'd made in her whole life. Until this moment, all her actions had undoubtedly been dictated by any number of masters and mistresses. But now, free to choose her own path, she chose to follow God's word. She counted on it. Because of that, she was able to turn and go back to serve a woman who didn't even like the sight of her.

How did she do it?

I believe that, when Hagar opened her heart to the angel's message, she was given another gift, one of wisdom and insight: In returning to Sarah, she was not really submitting to an unhappy, jealous, bossy woman; she was placing her life, troubles and all, in the hands of God. And that position gave her protection, favor and peace. She knew God's word for her and her child would never fail.

Do you understand what I'm telling you? Hagar saw the sovereignty of God. Sure, life had dealt her a rotten hand, so to speak. She wasn't a Jew, a child of the promise, and the baby she was carrying was someone else's bad idea. But now she knew God's unfailing love.

In fact, life for Hagar wasn't easy when she got back to Abraham's camp. Because of jealousy, Sarah would later have her and Ishmael driven back out into the desert, where the little boy would almost die of thirst. Even then, Hagar never forgot whom to call upon: the God whose eye was ever watching over her.

Hagar had come to rest on the solid rock of God's word to her: "Ishmael will be a great nation." She clung to that promise, knowing that under His watchcare nothing could crush or destroy them.

Recently I heard a story about a young Christian woman, whom I'll call Jenna. It gives further light on the biblical principles revealed in Hagar's story. In some ways, their stories are parallel.

As a young woman, Jenna's mother had lived in a roach-infested ghetto of a major city on the East Coast. She had fallen in love with and married a young, blue-collar worker who had abandoned her the moment she had said she was pregnant with his first child.

Alone, pregnant, jobless and unskilled, Jenna's

mother had sat on the fire escape of her tenement, cradling her growing tummy—weeping and praying.

Friends had laid some heavy counsel on Jenna's mother. "If you ever want to get out of this stinkin' hole, there's only one thing for you to do: Get an abortion. What chance does this baby have anyway? Get on with your life. Forget you ever married that jerk. Get some schooling, find a good job and start your life over."

But, while praying, Jenna's mother believed God had spoken to her heart. Deep inside, she'd heard His promise: "Give this child to Me. It won't be easy. But it will be all right. This child will grow up to be Mine."

True, it was a hard road. Scrubbing floors and emptying trash cans in office buildings isn't exactly a fairy-tale existence.

But I want to tell you: Today Jenna is a sharp administrator, serving the Lord in a four-thousand-member metropolitan church. Besides having experienced the privilege of leading her mother to an even deeper walk with the Lord, she spends a lot of her time counseling and teaching other young women who grew up on the same harsh, urban streets as she did.

"I wouldn't even be here," says Jenna, with tears in her eyes, "if my mother had listened to her 'friends' instead of obeying God's word."

How about you?

Is your job, your marriage or some other aspect of life just too unbearable? Or do you feel as if you missed

God somewhere? That your life is wrecked and now you're stuck in a dreary, second-best kind of existence?

Don't run from life. Run to God!

He may not give you a glimpse of His further plan, the way He revealed Ishmael's future to Hagar. He asks only that we take the first step, that we trust in Him, knowing that He is a God who longs to give hope to the hopeless.

As the Lord declared, through the prophet Jeremiah (who, by the way, faced some pretty awful situations himself): "For I know the plans I have for you...plans to prosper you and not to harm you, plans to give you hope and a future" (Jer. 29:11).

God's further word to you and me through Jeremiah reflects what we've already learned from Hagar's experience: "Call upon me and come and pray to me, and I will listen to you....Seek me with all your heart. I will be found by you...and will bring you back from captivity" (vv. 12-14).

God wants you free from everything that's binding you. But if you submit to Him only when people and circumstances are good, you won't gain much. You see, God always blesses when we put our lives in His hands—especially when things look the worst. Even if your life seems second-best, God has no trouble making the best of second-best. He always has a back-up plan.

Why not take every circumstance that's weighing you down and, right now in prayer, lay it in His hands?

When you take this first step and trust Him in your darkest moment, you're laying a foundation stone of faith that you can stand on and you will not be moved.

Then turn around and take a good look at that wall you've been up against.

You'll wonder how you ever mistook this heap of stones—that's no more than rubble—for a solid wall.

THREE

Esther: Fire That Doesn't Burn

One of the most popular Bible verses Christians love to quote is this ringing affirmation from the apostle Paul: "In all these things we are more than conquerors through him who loved us" (Rom. 8:37).

What a great promise—one of my favorites: We are more than conquerors!

Why is it, then, that many of us can quote this verse by rote, the way grade-school children rattle off the ABCs, and yet we so often slump along in defeat? We feel defeated at home, in our jobs or in our spiritual lives. In church or at a Christian conference, while the praise songs are wafting through the air, we're on top of the world, but then a fiery trial comes along, and we drop into the ashes.

It's hard to figure, especially when this great promise comes hot on the heels of another amazing statement of faith: "We know that in all things God works for the good of those who love him, who have been called according to his purpose" (Rom. 8:28).

That's a pretty fantastic promise, don't you think? And it's one we toss around with hardly a second thought.

I've come to believe that you and I have to pass through some kind of process for God's word to become real in our lives. Somehow, this word has to travel from our heads down into our hearts, so that we become conquerors.

Learning—the Hard Way!

There are some things I can just jump right in and trust God for. Finances, for instance. With an international ministry and a large church—not to mention the usual, personal, financial needs—Wally and I surely have been put to the test on many occasions. I won't say it's been a piece of cake, but I've discovered over the years that God is completely able to provide for us when we're doing His will. I've learned to arm myself with scriptural promises.

But when it came to our children—now that was another story. We'd always raised our son and daughter, Michael and Sarah, to have some measure of independence. But once they reached the age when it was time to leave the nest, well, my spiritual armor started to show some cracks.

I can surely sympathize with parents who become stricken with fear about their children. You raise a child through colds, fevers, cuts, scratches, emotional bumps and bruises. You do your best to love and discipline and encourage and give them every good opportunity, and then—!

Then they step out from the shelter of your love. And you just know the world isn't going to pour love on them the way you have.

Worse, every evening the news reports another horror story about serial killers, a drunk driver who's destroyed the life of an innocent person, new diseases. You name it—there's tragedy on every side! If you're not careful, every terrifying foot of videotape that's ever run on the six o'clock news will flash on the big-screen TV of your mind. Let your child be ten minutes late coming home, and you hit the panic button.

And, all the while, you know you have to let them go.

Believe me, I've never been a hovering mother. But, with all the junk that's going on in our world today, when Michael and Sarah were ready to leave home, I began to feel as fretting and flustered as an old mother hen. It wasn't that I didn't know what the Scriptures said about God's promises of love and protection. It's just that I was having a harder time than I thought getting those promises from my head down into my heart, where hidden fear was lurking.

One night in particular, God used Sarah to teach me a lesson.

I had decided to go to bed a little early, leaving Wally and Sarah still up. I turned out the light and, in a moment, was sound asleep.

A while later, though, I woke up. My mother's "antenna" was in operation. Shuffling downstairs, I noticed Wally was alone reading. "Where is Sarah?" I asked.

"Oh, she just drove down to the convenience store," he said casually. "She'll be back in a little while." Then he went back to his book.

When I returned to my room, the bedside clock said 10:30. A little late to be out alone, I thought. But Sarah was twenty-one, after all.

I would *not* be a worrisome mother.

I went to bed and turned out the light. Then I lay there wide awake, staring at the ceiling. Every time I heard a car coming down the street I'd tense up, hoping it would turn in. But each one passed.

The clock soon said eleven. All kinds of things can happen to a young woman late at night, I thought. And one by one each terrible predicament paraded in full color through my mind.

I couldn't stand it anymore! Jumping out of bed, I slid my feet into slippers, pulled on a bathrobe and was out in the car.

Half-ducking so no one would see me in my present state, I maneuvered the dark streets like a private detective on the prowl. My mind would alternately say, Maybe she's just had a flat tire, then, Oh, I know it's something terrible!

Then I spotted her—driving down the opposite side of the street. She passed by. Whew! I breathed a quick sigh of relief. She didn't see me. I turned around and hurried home, hoping to arrive before she did. But wouldn't you know—Sarah and I pulled into the driveway at the exact same moment!

Sarah came over to the car. I could see at once she was upset. "Mother, *what* are you doing out at this hour? You were looking for me, weren't you?"

I smiled weakly and tried to act as if I always drove around town in my bathrobe at night! Then I gave her one of those Mom-was-just-concerned-about-you-honey kind of replies.

But she wasn't buying it. More than that, the Lord used her to confront me with a personally tailored word.

"Mother," Sarah said, staring me in the eye, "you are supposed to be a person of faith. You teach it and talk about it all the time. You're always telling people to trust God in all things. And now—look at you. I can't believe that I couldn't go out on my own for one

37

hour without your getting so upset you had to come looking for me!''

Oh, how that hurt! Because she was right. Worst of all, the last people on earth you want to fail as a Christian are your own children. And, boy, had I ever blown it!

Sarah forgave me for that one. She and Michael are gracious that way.

But, after that, I started to pray and ask the Lord to show me how to become ''more than a conqueror'' over this kind of fear.

In response, the Holy Spirit showed me some deeper truths from the life of a Bible heroine I thought I knew pretty well. (That's always the way, isn't it? Just when you think you've got some part of the Bible figured out, along comes the Lord and shows you deeper meaning!)

The woman who drew my attention was Esther. Through her life I saw the process that God takes us through to cleanse us of spiritual impurities. He wants us to go from knowing His word, that is, saying we believe it, to putting it into practice.

Esther, a Jewess who became queen of Persia, might have lived a life of total luxury and ease. All her Jewish teachings could have stayed tucked away in her head. Everything she knew about God could have stayed locked in her cranium, where it would have been totally useless in helping her conquer any of the trials she would face. And there were many.

But then God's word came to her.

Take a careful look with me at how Esther's life was transformed.

As women in the Bible go, Esther is almost the opposite of Hagar. If Hagar was down-and-out, Esther was up-and-in. Hagar was sold into servitude, but Esther was a poor, orphaned, Jewish girl who wound up married to the king of the powerful Persian empire. Sounds like a fairy tale!

Another big difference is that Hagar was backed against a wall, so to speak. Esther had everything a girl could ever want, including glamor and stature. Yet how interesting that God used even this "cushy" position to change her!

The same may be true for some Christians today. It may be that you enjoy a good income, good health, well-behaved kids and a pretty good marriage. But God always has more! How much you receive depends on how settled in and self-satisfied you are.

While Esther was doing OK, however, the Jewish people as a whole were living through one of the darkest times in their history. After the Babylonians had conquered Israel, the Persians swept through and destroyed Babylon. That meant the Israelites were in a deeper hole than before.

The Persian kings ruled with an iron fist. Once a king made a law or a decree, that was it. Even he couldn't change or retract his own words. The king who conquered Babylon, Ahasuerus (A-has-u-e'-rus), ruled over the 127 provinces of Persia and Media, which extended from India to Ethiopia. He was one powerful and dangerous man, the kind of guy nobody dared to cross!

King Ahasuerus was something of a megalomaniac. Holding absolute, dictatorial control of most of the known world wasn't enough for this guy. He wanted to conquer Greece, too. So, to get the most military support possible, he called together all the leaders of his provinces.

As Esther's story opens, the king is throwing a lavish six-month party at his palace in Susa. The Bible says his palace was appointed in gold and silver, and each man drank from a specially fashioned, gold vessel. Talk about a gaudy display of wealth!

To top off this big bash, the king held a seven-day feast. One evening, when he was really drunk, he began to brag about his grand collection of beautiful objects from all over the world. Someone mentioned that his queen, Vashti, was reputed to be quite a knock-out.

The king must have leered with pride at the mention of his glamorous wife. In order to show her off—and to show her total obedience to him—he sent word for her to come immediately to his court wearing her crown and, some have suggested, nothing else.

You can imagine this egocentric king's embarrassment and anger when the chamberlain delivered Vashti's reply, which was in essence: "I have no intention of parading myself in front of you and your drunken friends!"

Furious, the king consulted with his seven princely wise men. One of them gave this advice: "Dump Vashti, quick! Or every woman in the kingdom will rebel against her husband's orders!"

So Vashti got the boot, and the king ordered his officials to hold the first, recorded beauty pageant to find her replacement. Hundreds of young virgins from all over the kingdom were brought to Susa and given the standard Persian beauty treatment, which meant a full year of preparation with scented baths, exotic skin oils, hair dressing and outfitting. (And some men today get upset when their wives spend a couple of hours a month in a beauty shop!)

While the king's men combed the kingdom for eligible young ladies, Mordecai, Esther's guardian, must have known his young charge would be among the girls chosen. He also knew she'd fare much better if her ancestry was disguised. So, instead of her Jewish name, Hadasseh, meaning "myrtle tree," he gave her the Persian name Esther, which means "star."

What a prophetic name! As Esther was escorted to the palace at Susa, neither she nor Mordecai could have imagined the great darkness in which this star would have to shine.

Well, the long and short of the story is this: After the year of preparation, King Ahasuerus had the lovely young women brought in—dozens and dozens of them. But only one stopped the show. We read, "The king was attracted to Esther more than to any of the other women, and she won his favor and approval more than any of the other virgins. So he set a royal crown on her head and made her queen instead of Vashti" (Esth. 2:17).

All this detail is important for several reasons. First, it sets the stage for God's working in Esther's life. Moreover, it says something to you and me: God is always at work behind the scenes, arranging the events of my life and yours so that He can do His deepest work in our hearts.

Now think about Esther for a moment. This girl, the orphan of Hebrew slaves, was crowned queen of the whole empire! The king gave a banquet in her honor, lavished her with gifts and declared a holiday to celebrate the beautiful new wife he'd chosen.

How many of us, hearing this story, are tempted to think, Boy, was she ever sitting pretty! But when Esther stepped onto the pages of Bible history as a queen, she wasn't like Snow White riding off with her prince into the sunset. For Esther, the story was just beginning.

Immediately, her situation became treacherous.

Shortly after Esther was crowned, Mordecai learned of a secret plot. Because the king's highest official, Haman, felt that Mordecai had slighted him, he became possessed with a satanic sort of rage. It wasn't enough to have Mordecai killed; Haman persuaded the king to order the annihilation of every Jewish man, woman and child in the whole kingdom. It was an unchangeable law!

Letters were drafted, sealed with the king's insignia. As far as Haman was concerned, the fate of the Jews was also sealed—but Mordecai caught wind of the plan.

It's at this moment that the word of God came to Esther.

Mordecai informed Esther about the plot, sending her a message: "Esther, you are the one who can go into the king's presence to beg mercy and plead with him for our people" (see Esth. 4:8).

And what was Esther's natural response?

The same as yours and mine is so often. She took a look at all the facts—by that I mean the external circumstances—and she flinched. The king didn't know that she was a Jew. That fact had been kept a secret. If she did what Mordecai asked, she'd blow her cover. You can almost hear the fear in her voice as she sent word back to Mordecai.

In essence she said: "Go and talk to the king? You've got to be kidding! Don't you remember how I got this job as queen in the first place? Remember what happened to Vashti when she refused a request in front of all those princes? And now you want me to ask the king to withdraw one of his laws after it's gone out to each one of those same princes all across the land?

"Besides," she went on, "you probably didn't know about this other law. It's a real doozy: If anyone whom the king hasn't asked to see approaches him, the penalty is death. The only thing that can save you is if he's in a good mood. If so, he'll hold out his scepter to you. If not, you're finished!"

Mordecai's comeback is a classic:

> Do not think that because you are in the king's house you alone of all the Jews will escape. For if you remain silent at this time, relief and deliverance for the Jews will arise from another place, but you...will perish.

Then catch this:

> And who knows but that you have come to royal position for such a time as this? (Esth. 4:13-14).

Now you and I most likely will never be in a position to use our influence to save a whole nation. But we are constantly placed in positions that are similar to Esther's.

No doubt you face decisions big and small every day that call for a specific choice. I know I do. And here's the choice: to give in to your natural inclinations or to draw on the word of God that you already know.

I'm sure that Esther grew up hearing all the exciting, miraculous stories of the patriarchs. She'd heard every detail of the Israelites' exodus from Egypt—the parting of the Red Sea, the miracle of manna from heaven. She'd probably learned by heart the song Hannah sang after miraculously conceiving and birthing Samuel.

And now Esther found herself thrust into a spot

where faith had to become reality. Another way to say this is that she had to decide which would control her actions: fear or faith.

Let me point out that Esther did some other important things before she risked approaching the king.

Esther acknowledged that God just might have a purpose in making her queen. She didn't say, "Oh yes. Now I see why God has placed me here," yet she did present a plan!

Esther said, "All right. I'll fast for three days—I and all the young maidens who attend me. Mordecai, you and all the Jews in Susa should fast, too."

In other words, Esther chose to handle this awful predicament in a spiritual way. She caught herself slipping into fear, and she made a decision. She knew the king had the power to kill her, yet she said, "After we fast, I will go" (see Esth. 4:15-16).

Here's the quick round-up of the story: Esther's intervention did save the Jews from annihilation. The satanic Haman was hanged instead. Mordecai was honored with a position second only to the king. And Esther went down in Bible history as one brave lady.

Once these facts are shaken aside, though, there's some spiritual gold left for you and me. 🖌

He Is Like a Purifying Fire

Esther had to be put through a trial before the truth of God's word could become real in her life. Spiritual impurities had to go. What were they? Fear and unbelief, among others.

Esther's story—coupled with my late-night experience with Sarah—showed me once again that spiritual growth is a process. And, quite often, that process involves heat! We know that gold has to be purified by fire. Only in fire can the dross be burned away.

In a similar way, God might allow our circumstances to become uncomfortably warm—even hot! Why? It's not that He wants to punish us or to see us jump and twitch as we dangle over the flames. But He knows that fiery circumstances will reveal impurities in our faith that we may never have seen before.

Impurity in our spirits is the source of so many of our problems. But as Christians we can rest assured: God has no intention of leaving us in that weak condition.

The book of Hebrews says,

> But Christ is faithful [as the builder of God's house]. And we are his house *if we hold on to our courage and the hope of which we boast...*
> See to it, brothers, that none of you has a sinful, unbelieving heart that turns away from the living God (Heb. 3:6,12, italics mine).

Jesus said, "The work of God is to believe on the one God sent" (see John 6:29). Of course He meant Himself—the living Word of God, the One in whom all of God's promises are "yes and amen" (see 2 Cor. 1:20).

After studying the story of Esther, I decided to learn a lesson from the night I blew it with Sarah. Instead of just being mortified because I'd gotten overheated about her welfare, I chose to see that experience as a little bit of purifying heat from God. Like Esther, I'd sought God. And He had exposed a pocket of fear and unbelief in me.

The result was that I asked His forgiveness and asked Him to help me place fuller trust in His promise to watch over all that concerns me. Just listen to this:

> Though I walk in the midst of trouble, thou wilt revive me...and thy right hand shall save me. The Lord will perfect that which concerneth me (Ps. 138:7-8, KJV).

You, too, can walk through life with that victorious spirit—even "in the midst of trouble." But that spirit won't be revealed in you until you face some fiery trials. Those trials are not meant to burn and destroy you; they're meant to bring to light your doubt and anxiety.

Don't let your doubts and heartaches and anxieties turn you away from God. When trouble comes, turn toward Him.

Then God's fire will clean away the dross. And you will wind up much stronger than before, with a faith in Him and His word that is pure and strong.

Like Esther, you can receive God's word to you— even in the midst of the darkest moment of your personal history—and you can come out shining like gold!

FOUR

Eli: Meeting
the God Who Loves

Sometimes I get delighted when I'm studying about the men and women of the Bible. What excites me most is the way their stories reveal the heart and character of God.

Over and over again He appears throughout Scripture as a sort of "master weaver," threading together events and personalities to bring about His perfect plan.

We've already seen how Hagar was brought through servitude and humiliation to reveal God's watch-care for people who are without hope. (And do I ever cling to *that* when events pile up against me!) Esther was given a crown in a heathen kingdom, so that the word hidden in her heart could break forth and bring deliverance to thousands of Jewish people.

And yet there are others in the Bible whose lives reveal God's word of solemn warning. Yes, God comes to each of us in a personal way, with a word that will direct, purify and reveal His plan through our lives. But because you and I each have a free will, we can choose to turn that word away.

To be flat-out honest, though, I find as much encouragement even from the lives of the Bible's "bad" examples as from the good. The reason is this: I'm certainly not exempt from missing God, just as some of these people ignored His word. But because I know God's intention toward me is always good, I can listen to His warning to them; that way I can avoid making the same mistake myself.

It's beautiful when you see God as He is; even in the way He warns us, His tremendous love is revealed. It all depends on what you focus upon.

One man whose life demonstrates God's warning love is Eli, who abused his priesthood and brought trouble to his own house for generations. Perhaps you've already read his story, found at the beginning of 1 Samuel, and focused only on the judgment that came upon Eli and his sons for their evil deeds. But take another look at this story with new eyes—focusing on God and not just on Eli—and I think you'll be blessed by what you see.

Eli Was a Mixture

Eli lived at Shiloh, where the house of the Lord stood before Solomon built the great temple in Jerusalem. Probably the house of the Lord mentioned in 1 Samuel 1 was the wilderness tabernacle, which Moses, Aaron and the Levites built at God's command during the exodus from Egypt. It found a more or less permanent resting place at Shiloh, which was in the hill country north of Jerusalem and overlooking the Jordan River valley.

It was always God's plan to lead the people through His priests, never through a king (see 1 Sam. 8:4-9). So God wanted His priests to live holy lives and teach their children to obey God's commands and ordinances. This was very important, because the priest's sons served right at his side and, when the high priest died, his oldest son inherited his place of leadership. So the priest's duties included training his sons in reverence and godliness.

Unfortunately, the office of fatherhood is where Eli's biggest flaws showed up, with glaring highlights! His sons, Hophni and Phinehas, were a tragedy waiting to happen.

The first thing that we learn about Eli is that he lived by a *double standard*.

Just look at what happened when Hannah accompanied her husband, Elkanah, from their home in

Ramah up to Shiloh to present their annual sacrifice.

The Bible tells us that Hannah was barren. Even though this grieved her deeply, she didn't wallow in self-pity. She knew what to do! While Elkanah was delivering the sacrifice for his family, Hannah went before the Lord in prayer. Her sacrifice to God came in the form of a vow.

"God," she said, "if You will give me a son, I will give him back to You for all the days of his life!" (see 1 Sam. 1:11). She was in deep sorrow, weeping and praying silently in her heart, though her lips were moving.

Just then, Eli spotted her. All he could see was a woman swaying back and forth, her eyes swollen and red, her hair disheveled. He jumped to conclusions. "How long will you keep getting drunk? Get rid of your wine" (v. 14).

Hannah was not tipsy with wine, of course, and she politely told him so. Even though he'd called her a drunk, she addressed him respectfully, saying, "Not so, my lord" (v. 15).

Now stop and think about this small incident for a moment. It says something to me about Eli. His spiritual vision was already greatly impaired. He couldn't tell the difference between a heartfelt cry to God and a drunken stupor! It's interesting that his physical eyesight also became so weak that he could hardly see (see 1 Sam. 3:2).

But more important, Eli's rebuke to Hannah reveals

something deeper about his character. Eli's standard of godliness wasn't exactly pure, for he falsely accused Hannah but allowed his sons to bring shame to God. "Eli's sons were wicked men; they had no regard for the Lord" (1 Sam. 2:12). When men came bringing animal sacrifices, Hophni and Phinehas stole the meat right out of their hands! If anyone resisted, they threatened him with a beating.

And what was Eli's response? He was only worried about the bad report that was spreading among the people (v. 24). Compare him with Aaron, who loved the Lord so much he continued to serve Him even after his two sons were killed for offering "strange fire" on God's altar (see Lev. 10).

Eli's double standard was bad enough. But there was another "mixed match" going on in his spirit.

Eli was double-minded in his faith.

When Hannah told Eli she had been praying in anguish and grief, he had enough spiritual sensitivity to speak a powerful word of faith to her. "Go in peace," he said, "and God will grant your request" (see 1 Sam. 1:17).

Yet he showed no spiritual insight at all when it came to his sons' abuse of their office. Eli could have had his sons physically removed from the tabernacle if he'd wanted to. But he evidently made no move to stop their crime against God. Again, Eli's relationship to his sons reveals something about his spiritual condition, so that God said of Eli, "You scorn my sacrifice and offering" (1 Sam. 2:29).

Odd, isn't it? Eli was able to see Hannah through the eyes of faith, but he was unable to see the enormity of his sons' sins or of his own.

But think twice before you judge Eli as evil. I know that I am a mixture. Aren't you?

I've known Christian leaders who preach with power, and countless lives are changed. Then they go home—where they're difficult to live with. There are generous, loving Christians who would literally give you the shirt off their back and the bed they sleep on—but they can't whittle off the extra forty pounds they're carrying because they can't pass up a chocolate bar (or two). What about the young Christian who loves God so much he's willing to give his life to ministry or missions—but he struggles continually with a lustful imagination?

The list could go on and on. The gentle Christian "mother-type" who has a gift for helping—though she sometimes crosses the line into meddling. And what about the promises and offers of help we make, with every good intention, only to find later that we don't even *want* to live up to our word?

And what about more serious matters? What about the Christian businessman who, against his better judgment, enters into that one shady deal? What about the wife and mother who lets her emotions carry her away into an affair? What about when we wrongly accuse, slander or gossip about a friend?

Sometimes even the best Christian can blow it big-time!

The truth is, most of us are a mixture of strengths and weaknesses. The person who thinks that being born again means instant, sinless perfection is in for a rough time. And the person who sees things only in black and white (the kind who says, "Either Jesus is Lord *of* all, or He can't be your Lord *at* all") usually makes it hard on everyone else.

Personally, I can identify with Paul, especially when he was in the frame of mind to pen these honest words: "I do not understand what I do. For what I want to do I do not do, but what I hate I do" (Rom. 7:15). Paul was talking about the problem of mixture—of being a Christian who *wants* to please God but finds himself sinning again and again.

Now when we finally see that we're double-minded, just like Eli, is that the end of it as far as God is concerned? Does He shake His head and say, "You're not holy enough for Me. You say you believe in Me and want to follow Me, but your faith *leaks*"?

No way! God wants you to come to Him with the most honest prayer of your heart, even if it's the prayer of the man who cried out to Jesus, "I do believe; help me overcome my unbelief!" (Mark 9:24).

Sometimes God will send His word to confront us. He offers us every chance to turn from the unbelief that blocks His life in us and leads us away from Him. Not only that, but He's incredibly creative in the way He speaks to us.

Just look at the amazing ways God sent His word to Eli.

First, God spoke to Eli through the life of Samuel.

While Samuel was still a little boy, just barely weaned, Hannah set off once again for Shiloh. She said, "I vowed to give this child to the Lord. So now here he is. His whole life will be given over to the Lord" (see 1 Sam. 1:28).

Hannah wasn't the kind to say, "Well, Lord, I know I promised my child to You *then*. But that was before I knew what it was like to hold a child in my arms and look into his precious little face. Surely You don't want me to live up to that silly little vow!" No, Hannah was single-minded.

And so Hannah arrived on Eli's doorstep one day to hand over young Samuel into Eli's care. Then she turned her back to leave. It's not hard to imagine the boy crying, reaching out for his mother. Think how that must have pricked Eli's heart. What a dramatic way for the Lord to point out Eli's sin. This woman had just turned her baby over to the Lord—while Eli's two, big lugs were outside harassing the worshippers and profaning the Lord's name.

Then there was the *way* Samuel ministered before the Lord.

It's pretty obvious that Eli's ministry was done "in the flesh." It was routine and not too spiritual, for, we read, "in those days the word of the Lord was rare;

there were not many visions" (1 Sam. 3:1).

Yet Scripture says of Samuel, he "continued to grow in stature and in favor with the Lord and with men" (1 Sam. 2:26). He was so favored by God that men were drawn to him. The Bible says that of only one other man in all history—Jesus! Think how Eli must have felt looking at his own sons. Everywhere he turned, he heard the people murmuring evil reports about their great sinfulness.

The second way the word of God came to Eli was through *direct confrontation* by the Lord.

To Eli the Lord sent a prophet who said, "Why do you honor your sons more than me by fattening yourselves on the choice parts of every offering made by my people Israel?" (1 Sam. 2:29).

Boy, did that prophet ever hit the nail on the head! He nailed Eli's two biggest problems: He respected his sons' desires more than the Lord's; and he loved food—that is, he catered to his own stomach. (In 1 Samuel 4:18 we read that Eli was so fat that when he fell off a chair he broke his neck and died.)

Eli did not know how to walk by faith. He walked by sight. The flesh was much more real to him than the Spirit of God, and he apparently did nothing to seek God out and learn of His ways. So he became fat and lazy and a terrible example to his sons, who grew up just like their father.

But the Lord loved Eli! Why else would He have gone to such great lengths to warn him? If Eli had heeded that word, he could have turned from his own sin and put an end to his sons' evil practices. But he did not.

And so the word of the Lord came to Eli a second time, now through the little boy Samuel. God said, in effect, "I loved you and gave you a chance, Eli. But you didn't bother to listen. And so all that I warned you about is going to come to pass!" (see 1 Sam. 3:11-14).

Who knows what the Lord would have done if Eli had willingly turned, even at the last minute. But he took a lazy attitude, shrugged and said, "Let the Lord do whatever is good in His eyes" (see v. 18).

Most important to you and me is this: The whole story speaks volumes about God's love. He never lets the ceiling drop in on our heads without first giving us a loud warning. Eli could have repented. And then God went and gave him a second chance!

Is there something in your life the Lord is speaking to you about? Corrections He wants you to make? Actions He wants you to stop? Relationships that need to change? Promises to fulfill?

You may be thinking, I want to do what the Lord wants—what I know is right. But I just can't. I don't have it in me. I've even set out to make changes. Then I fall flat on my face again.

If so, at least you're in good company—with the apostle Paul and millions of other Christians.

There is a way for you and me to escape from the

double-mindedness that holds us down in a weakened spiritual condition and leaves us open to all sorts of attacks.

The first thing we need to do is get rid of the ho-hum, so-what-else-is-new? attitude toward sin and defeat. As Paul said, "God is faithful; he will not let you be tempted beyond what you can bear....he will also provide a way out so that you can stand up under it" (1 Cor. 10:13).

So many times I run into people who are troubled by this Scripture passage. "What's the 'way' Paul was talking about?" they ask. "Why didn't he make it clear?"

He did. The way of escape from sin and spiritual waffling is revealed in the very next verse: "Therefore, my dear friends, flee from every idolatry" (v. 14). Ouch! Idolatry? Me?

Yes, I hate to break the news to you, but sometimes you and I fall prey to the sin of idolatry—just like Eli.

We've seen that the crux of Eli's problem was that he esteemed his sons more than the Lord. In other words, it was more important for him to hear them say, "Gee, what a good father you are; you let us get away with anything we want," than to hear the Lord say, "Well done, good and faithful servant!"

To *esteem* something or someone means to set your eyes upon it—to lift it up to a position of high honor. Eli was more willing to offend God than to offend his sons by rebuking them.

59

This is where the account of God's warning to Eli gets a little scary for you and me.

Today, it's popular to spend a lot of time looking for the emotional roots of sins. I don't say those roots are not there. But there's always another question we have to face: What is it that you esteem more than God? What do you set your eyes upon, to lift up and honor above Him?

Some people honor *hard evidence* above God and His word. These are the folks who say, "I won't believe it until I see it!"

Some people esteem their *possessions* more than God. They're like the rich young ruler (Matt. 19:16-24), who couldn't let go of his wealth to trust God for provision. His motto was something like "One in the hand is worth fifty in the bush!"

Many Christians hear testimony after testimony about God's miraculous provision and still say secretly in their hearts, "I hope God doesn't ask me to trust Him like that!" Their underneath attitude is unbelief: God's word may say He will provide, but I don't believe He'll provide *exactly what I like*! So, when a time of financial shortage comes, they hit the panic button. Or God asks them to step out on faith and they say, "No way!" Can you see how this is idolatry?

For others the idol is *reputation*. "I know God wants me to witness to my neighbor, but she'll think I'm a fanatic." In no way do I mean to place a burden of guilt on anyone—because God motivates through love and conviction—but there are many unbelievers who live next door to Christians who esteem their reputation above God and remain silent.

You see, God loved Eli so much that He sent several fair warnings, pleading with him to turn away from his two false idols: his sons and his fleshly comforts.

I know a young man, whom I'll call Dan, who had to come to terms with an idol in his life.

Dan is a Christian, and he grew up with a great love for the family. As a teenager, he especially admired Jim, his youth group leader, and the way Jim involved his whole family in serving the Lord. In his heart Dan prayed and said, "Lord, someday I'm going to have a family that's going to be just like that."

In a few years Dan met and married a beautiful Christian woman. In a short time they had a sweet, bright-eyed boy, named Eric. Before the little guy was a year old, Dan ran out and bought fishing poles and train sets. Every night he prayed over Eric, giving him to the Lord for His service. This little guy was the pride and joy of his daddy!

Then, when Eric was only two, he suddenly developed asthma. Sometimes the attacks were severe. His chest would heave as he gasped for breath. He would lie in his daddy's arms and cry out, "Dear Jesus, help me!" That cut Dan's heart the deepest.

Dan and his wife prayed in faith, believing God could heal Eric. But inwardly Dan also thought, My son is begging You, Lord! Can't You help him?

One night Dan and his wife were awakened to the sounds of choking coming from Eric's room. Dan rushed through the dark, while his wife reached for the phone to call the local emergency room.

When Dan switched on the light in Eric's room, the sight shocked him. Eric was out of bed, lying on the bedroom floor, drenched in sweat. He'd obviously been laboring for breath for some time, unable even to cry out for help. His face was a dusky blue, indicating lack of oxygen to the blood, and his lips were nearly purple.

As Dan scooped his son's limp body into his arms, the little boy looked him in the eyes and whispered, "Why won't God help me?"

Dan says he felt anger blaze through him, like a bolt of lightning through his chest. Silently, he shot a furious charge at God: If You can't heal my son, then You aren't God; You're a fraud and a liar! And if You let him die I'll curse You!

Dan was able to get Eric to the hospital in time. The doctors were able to save his life.

Once Eric was peacefully asleep in a hospital bed, Dan found himself alone. At once, he was confronted with the enormity of what he'd said to God. More important, though, he realized what God was saying to him.

"As I sat there looking at Eric," Dan says, "it was as if God was saying to me, 'Dan, Eric is an idol to you. You love him far more than you love Me. Because of that, you can't trust his life and well-being into My hands. You don't think I'll care for him the way you think he should be cared for.'

"God didn't make Eric sick to teach us a lesson," Dan insists. "But He did use the asthma to reveal to me that I'd placed Eric before Him."

Just like Eli, Dan had lifted up his son above the Lord.

"Once I confessed that sin," says Dan, "a tremendous peace just washed all through me. Then came the assurance that, no matter what, God does love Eric and has the best in mind for him. But God is first, no matter what."

After that night, though Eric's asthma continued to flare up for some time, Dan says the peace never left. He could always look back to the time when God used even a frightening, life-threatening situation to get Dan's focus right again.

It's so easy to get our eyes off God—to put other things before Him. This world is so real, surrounded as we are by people, places and things we love and depend upon. God can seem distant and vague and *not* real sometimes. I guess that's why He warned us, saying, "Don't allow any false gods to come before me" (see Ex. 20:3)—not even father or mother, brother or sister, wife or husband, children or any possession (see Luke 14:26).

It's not that God doesn't understand or approve of our love for one another, our joy in beautiful things. It's just that putting those things before Him leads to spiritual death. Only He can give us real joy. He is the God of life. When we put Him first, above all else, He will give us the abundant life we seek.

Has God's word revealed something in your heart that you esteem above Him? A friend? Your career? Even a spiritual gift that gives you stature among fellow Christians? Some people say, "Well, even if everything's not right in my life, God still loves me." I say, Yes, He loves you; He loves you too much to have you under bondage to false gods of your own making!

Why not take inventory right now? Lay everything in your life at His feet in prayer. Have you been resting your life on things you can see—people and possessions—and not on faith? Don't make the mistake Eli made; you can change your attitude! God reveals sin, not to condemn or hurt you, but so you can be renewed in His love.

I promise you. Once you've made Him Master of your house and all you own, trusting Him with everything you hold dear, you'll find that He is absolutely trustworthy. He is the God who loves.

I know that God has made a way for me to change, which Paul also revealed: "Do not conform any longer to the pattern of this world, but be transformed by the renewing of your mind" (Rom. 12:2).

FIVE

Elijah: Shining for God—or Burning Out?

R ecently I heard a story about a man with a brilliant public ministry—and his tragic secret life.

God's gifts really poured through this man, whom I'll call Mark. He had an unusual, spiritual sensitivity.

When people came to him with problems, he quickly had a supernatural "word of wisdom" that applied to their need. Time and time again, tough situations were turned around. There were times when men and women came to Mark for prayer, and God would give him a penetrating "word of knowledge" so that he could pinpoint secrets and thoughts of the heart.

Mark started with a small, personal ministry. But he soon became so well-known and respected that people clamored for him to go on the air.

Many said, "You need to be on a radio show—television, too. People out there need what you have to give." Mark resisted. Television and radio are very expensive. "Don't worry about the money," advisers assured him. "It'll come in." Mark went on the air.

For quite a while, the ministry grew in popularity. I'd heard about Mark and, occasionally, when I was traveling in his region, I'd turn on the TV and admire the Lord's ministry through him.

But after a time there were some warning signs. Nothing too obvious—just little things. A teaching that was a little "off center." A "word of wisdom" that seemed kind of strange.

About this time, I learned that Mark's ministry was faced with financial problems. But, by now, he had a staff and his ministry had grown popular, so he refused to cut back or go off the air. Money-wise, things continued to get worse.

Mark went to his pastor and said, "I'm going to start a church."

"Why on earth are you starting a church?" the pastor asked.

"Because I need the money for my TV and radio ministries," Mark replied.

"That's no reason to start a church!" the pastor retorted. "You've got to have a call from God to do that. Without it, you'll crash."

Mark did start the church. Immediately it boomed. Overnight it grew to around five hundred people.

Then, suddenly, it was discovered that Mark was involved in a secret love-affair. Not only did the church crash, but Mark crashed, too.

Why is this story so common today, and not just among popular Christian leaders? Why is it that so many everyday Christians seem to flame so brightly, only to burn out before our very eyes?

Before we focus on the negative (let's leave that to the news media!), I want to turn that question around: Why is it that some Christians seem to go from strong to stronger? What's *their* secret? What keeps them from suffering burnout?

Is it just that some folks are naturally bright and sunny? Do they simply let pressures roll off their backs? Do some people have an innate sense of pacing that tells them when to stop, rest and re-energize?

The ability to face life's challenges with an up attitude certainly is important. As Solomon observed, "A cheerful heart is good medicine" (Prov. 17:22). Likewise, it takes good sense to know when you're "burning the candle at both ends" and that your body, mind and spirit need a break.

But I believe there's more to avoiding burnout than that. You can keep a smile on your face (and even in

67

your heart) and you can schedule time off for loung-
ing on the beach or fishing and still crash physically
or, worse, spiritually. There are deeper, spiritual causes
that lead Christians into fatigue and, eventually, total
burnout.

One of the Bible's greatest men—Elijah—suffered
from a megadose of burnout. By examining his life,
I think you'll see one of the hidden, root causes of this
problem which affects so many of us today. And you'll
see the unusual way the word of God brought spiritual
restoration to Elijah.

The Fiery Prophet Who Burned Out

To understand Elijah's drive and something of what
made him tick, you need to get a view of Israel as he
saw it in his day.

King David had raised Israel to a position of strength
it had never before enjoyed. After him, of course, came
Solomon, whose wisdom and wealth were unequalled
among the ancient, Oriental kingdoms. Unfortunately
Solomon also opened the floodgates of ruin.

Solomon allowed some of his one thousand wives—
many of whom were heathen—to lead him into the
worship of false gods. Idols sprang up everywhere.
Immediately you can see the influence of the demonic
spirits which operated behind the stone idols. Israel
began to be torn apart.

Solomon's son Rehoboam was a spoiled brat who
demanded heavy taxes and hard labor from the people,

under threats of terrible punishment. Because of him, all the northern tribes of Israel rebelled against the throne. That left only Judah and the small tribe of Benjamin to rule the Southern Kingdom.

Not that the Northern Kingdom was any better without Rehoboam. The Northern Kingdom's first king, Jeroboam, introduced the worship of demon gods by setting up golden calves. (You want to ask: Didn't those people know their own history? Didn't they ever learn?) A succession of evil kings in both the Northern and Southern Kingdoms only made things worse.

So by Elijah's day, not only was Israel crippled in a military and political way, but its spiritual life was being torn apart by evil spiritual influences the way wolves tear apart young, unprotected lambs. I believe Elijah was so gifted with spiritual insight that God may actually have allowed him to glimpse these ravenous spirits that were thirsting for the souls of the Israelites.

Now Elijah had a tremendous love and zeal for the Lord—and a fiery personality to boot!

If anyone in history had a reformer's spirit, it was Elijah. It was his call and his mission to stand up against the decadence that had sunk the entire country in sin. However, there was one little problem.

Elijah had a powerful enemy—King Ahab. This guy was so crude and evil that the Bible says of him, "Ahab...did more to provoke the Lord, the God of Israel, to anger than did all the kings of Israel before him" (1 Kin. 16:33).

Actually, Ahab was kind of a sniveler. If he couldn't get his way, he did what any red-blooded king would do: He curled up in bed, turned his face to the wall and pouted (see 1 Kin. 21:1-4).

The real power behind the throne was someone much worse than Ahab. Her name was Jezebel, the queen. She was a Sidonian (see 1 Kin. 16:31). That meant she was from the combined kingdom of Tyre and Sidon, where they had perfected the vicious sacrifice of live babies by throwing them in a fire before an idol of Molech. So you can believe this lady was wide open to the power of demon spirits!

In fact, Jezebel would become such a symbol for evil that her name is actually associated with treachery and demon spirits in Revelation 2:20.

Remember, this couple I've just described were the king and queen of Israel! It's no wonder God called Elijah to the office of prophet. I believe that God always calls a prophet whose gifts match the prevailing evils of the day.

Ahab and Jezebel were sold out to do evil. They were dangerous in their cunning and the secret plots they whispered behind closed doors. Elijah, on the other hand, was unusually bold and outspoken for God. He was gifted with a faith that was boisterous and flamboyant.[9]

Just take a look at his strong spirit!

The 450 prophets of Baal and 400 prophets of

Asherah—men who ate at Jezebel's own table (see 1 Kin. 18:19)—had erected a huge shrine to their demon god and goddess on Mount Carmel. Notice how the enemy always tries to pick the highest point where he can stake his claim!

At that time, many of God's people were wavering between continuing to follow God or turning to Baal-worship. Elijah wasn't about to sit idly by; he drew the battle lines sharp and clear.

One day Elijah invited King Ahab and all the people of Israel to come out to Mount Carmel, where the 450 prophets of Baal held forth. Can you picture it? (See 1 Kin. 18:16-45.)

Ahab, Elijah's archenemy, was the first to speak. "So it's you, Elijah—you troublemaker!" Most likely Ahab was just waiting for his chance to seize Elijah and have him killed.

That didn't rattle Elijah one bit. He had a plan in mind that was going to knock Ahab's socks off!

Turning to the people of God, he really let them have it. "If our God is God, then follow Him! If you think Baal is God, then follow him! But quit being so wishy-washy!" Those people were either embarrassed or too afraid of Ahab to say anything. They froze and didn't say a word.

Next, Elijah challenged the prophets of Baal. "Get two bulls," he ordered them. "You take one, slay it and get it ready to sacrifice on your altar. But don't set it on fire."

71

Once the preparations were made, Elijah said, "Go ahead now. Call on Baal to light the fire supernaturally and burn up your sacrifice."

Those prophets took up the challenge. They danced around their altar from morning till noon, shouting, "O Baal, answer us!"

Elijah only laughed and taunted them. "Shout louder! Surely Baal is a god. Maybe he's in deep thought and hasn't heard you yet. Maybe he's just busy. Maybe he left home for a while!"

Imagine the boldness! One man against hundreds of angry, heathen priests!

Elijah's challenge sent the prophets of Baal into a frenzy. They cut themselves with spears and swords; they danced and screamed out to Baal while the blood ran down their bodies. All afternoon their madness mounted, until the time of the evening sacrifice.

Then Elijah stepped up. He prepared the altar for the burnt offering as usual. But wait—!

"Soak the sacrifice and the wood with water," Elijah instructed the people. "Not just once. Do it three times." Wet wasn't good enough. He wanted it soggy.

Once this was done, Elijah stepped up to the altar and cried out in a loud voice, so no one could miss it, "O Lord...let it be known today that you are God in Israel and that I am your servant!" (v. 36).

Talk about putting your faith on the line! But Elijah didn't have faith in his own power; he had faith in God.

Instantly, we read, "the fire of the Lord fell and burned up the sacrifice, the wood, the stones and the soil, and also licked up the water in the trench" (v. 38).

Then Elijah commanded God's people—who no longer had any question about whose side they were on!—to chase down the prophets of Baal and slay every one with the sword. No doubt Ahab cleared out quickly and hightailed it home with his tail between his legs.

A decisive victory for God, wouldn't you say?

Because Elijah was flamboyant and a risk taker, God could use him to confront the demon Baal out in the open, with hundreds of onlookers. Elijah was called upon because he was gifted with boldness in a time that required strong faith.

Then how do you explain Elijah's next move?

Once Ahab got home, he told Jezebel that Elijah had killed every one of her prophets. She was livid! "I vow by my gods that by this time tomorrow, Elijah will be a dead man!" (see 1 Kin. 19:1-2).

When Elijah caught wind of Jezebel's vow, the Bible says, he "was afraid and ran for his life" (v. 3). Out into the wilderness he ran, probably looking over his shoulder every step of the way, imagining the sound of pursuing hoofbeats. At one point, he even left his servant behind and ran on alone for a day.

Finally, he collapsed under a broom tree and despaired of life. The mighty prophet who had called down fire from heaven prayed to die! "Take my life," he cried to the Lord (v. 4). Then, exhausted, he lay down and fell asleep.

Aren't you glad God doesn't pay attention to some of your prayers? I surely am. We're so often ready to throw in the towel and quit—when God has just begun to work with us!

And that's the way it was with Elijah. You see, God was also at work in Elijah's life. He could certainly use that gift of boldness that ran through Elijah's nature like steel girders. But I believe God also wanted Elijah to become an even stronger, more useful servant. And that could mean only one thing: Elijah's natural giftings and character strengths had to take second place to something greater!

Earlier I told the story of Mark, the gifted young man with the powerful ministry. I suspect that he suffered burnout for the same reason that burnout overtook Elijah under that broom tree: Both men got their eyes off the Lord and focused instead on their own gifts.

Why do I say this? Look at the clues in Elijah's story.

When the people of God stood shaking in terror, refusing to stand up for the Lord, what did Elijah say? "I am the only one of the Lord's prophets left" (1 Kin. 18:22).

In other words, he was saying something like, "There's no one else who can or will do this job the way I can. If it weren't for me, who'd get the job done? It's all resting on my shoulders."

Can you hear the wrong attitude behind that?

It's so easy to get a martyr-complex. It's easy for us mothers to get into a mind-set that takes us spiralling downward: Look at all I do for my husband and kids— and what thanks do I get? If it weren't for me, this house would be condemned by the board of health. And my husband—huh! He couldn't balance the checkbook or scramble an egg if his life depended on it!

For Christians who are in leadership positions— whether leading a small Bible study or pastoring a large church—the inner grumblings are slightly different: Boy, these people have no idea how much I sacrifice for them! Most of them probably wouldn't care if they did realize it. But I can't abandon them. If I let someone else take over so I can have a breather, the people won't get the same quality of leadership that I give them.

Dads and husbands have their own set of internal gripes: I go off every day to slave at a job that I hate, for a boss who doesn't know his head from a hoe— and what thanks do I get? My wife expects me to be Mr. Romance when I get home after a hard day. And the kids don't even have time to say hi as they troop out the door, with their hands out for money and the car keys.

This kind of complaining opens the door for the enemy to come in. First, it fills your head with wrong desires. Then it allows you to justify your sin.

A complaining spirit can open the way for the tired mother or father to justify anger, hostility, selfishness and isolation from the family. It can lead the gifted and overworked minister to justify an affair.

Complaining is a signal that you are in danger of burnout. When you hear yourself complaining, it's like seeing the alternator light come on in your car—which means the engine is draining the battery. If you don't heed the warning, in a short time you'll be conked out on the side of the road, going nowhere!

You see, burnout happens when we stop depending on the Lord for our spiritual resource. Instead we draw on one of two other "power" sources.

One power source is our own human soul. Some of us are long on willpower, personality, natural gifts and the power of our emotions. Often we can rely on these things to get us through.

Unfortunately the reason we often mistakenly draw on this kind of energy is because of ego. Sometimes we enjoy hearing people say, "Boy, he's a gifted person. I've never known someone who's so strong and gifted in such-and-such."

In other words, we sometimes want the admiration of people more than we want to glorify the Lord. It's a weakness we all share in some measure.

Several years ago I met a man I'll call Al, who worked in the offices of a large church. From the moment Al opened his mouth, he talked only about the people who came to him for counsel. The way he talked, it almost sounded as if no one went to the pastor any more, because the pastor's advice was not quite as wise and spiritual as Al's.

Shortly thereafter, I met Al's pastor. When I mentioned Al and the impression he'd made on me, the pastor shook his head. "Al really does love people. He tries to be a spiritual father to them. But he doesn't counsel; he gets people to depend on him. He just needs to be needed."

I later learned that Al got exactly what he was after. A whole bunch of people had come to depend on him—so much that they called him morning, noon and night! Soon he couldn't stand up to the demand for his time and attention.

Because Al was fueled only by the power of his soul, and not by God's Spirit, he burned out.

God always wants to redirect us when our own egos become too outsized and get in His way. The amazing thing is that He does it kindly. ❦

Consider how gentle He was in changing Elijah's focus. Now I don't think Elijah's problem was all ego. I believe he had a strong dose of the second kind of power we often rely on: physical energy. He was a hard worker!

Listen to what an angel said to Elijah after he had slept for some time under the broom tree: "Get up and eat, for the journey is too much for you" (1 Kin. 19:7).

God knows that once we start running on our own energy, we can drain ourselves physically. We run ourselves ragged sometimes, thinking we're doing God a favor! But "he knows how we are formed; he remembers that we are dust" (Ps. 103:14). He kindly restores us, body and soul.

If you think God isn't at all interested in your taking care of your body, pay special attention to the Lord's concern for Elijah's physical well being, as described in 1 Kings 19. God wants you to shine, not burn out before He's accomplished His total plan for your life!

God wants His life to flow through you. That's why it's so important to learn how to draw your strength from His Spirit. Then His life in you will be like refreshing wells of living water that never go dry (see John 4:13-14).

How do you draw from the wells of His Spirit? That's what God taught Elijah when he reached his destination, Mount Horeb. That was when the word of the Lord came to him in the cave where he'd been sleeping.

We read, "The word of the Lord came to [Elijah]: 'What are you doing here?' " (1 Kin. 19:9).

The first thing God did was to let Elijah pour out his complaint. Elijah told Him all about the rotten things that had happened to him—what a hard worker he'd been, how nobody appreciated him, least of all Jezebel who was after his head!

God must have known Elijah was ready to get down to business now. So he sent him out to the mouth of the cave, saying, "I'm going to pass by you, Elijah!"

Imagine Elijah running out of the cave, clinging to that rocky mountainside, hoping for a glimpse of the Mighty, Invisible One of Israel!

> Then a great and powerful wind tore the moun-
> tains apart...but the Lord was not in the wind.
> After the wind there was an earthquake, but the
> Lord was not in the earthquake. After the earth-
> quake came a fire, but the Lord was not in the
> fire (vv. 11-12).

By this time, Elijah must have been thinking, Where
is God in all this noise and bluster?

It seems to me that's exactly what God wanted to
ask that flamboyant prophet: You've hit the nail on
the head, Elijah. You've got a lot of wind. You can
shake things up like an earthquake. And you surely
have the fire! But where am I in all this noise and
bluster?

In fact, God must have asked him something that hit
the nail on the head, because we read: "After the fire
came a gentle whisper" (v. 12).

Whatever God whispered to Elijah, we know it went
to the heart of his problem, for verse 13 says, "When
Elijah heard it, he pulled his cloak over his face."

Isn't that the way we react when God reveals our
hidden motives to us? What was God saying by coming to Elijah in a whisper?

He was saying, "Elijah, you've got a strong personality. You can intimidate people to death. Your faith can
call down fire. But if you rely on your flamboyant
personality, you're always going to wind up running
in fear—burned out and wanting to die—once your

79

limited human strength runs out.

"If you want the kind of staying power that will always get you through, you've got to get a rein on your natural gifts. You've got to quiet them down and learn to listen in the depths of your being for My still, small voice!"

That's what God wants to say to you and me today, too.

We can certainly be happy for the natural gifts, talents and character strengths God has blessed us with. But if we want to make it over the long haul, we've got to see that our strengths have an end. And His don't! When all our bluster and hard work run out, His strength is eternal. His power will never fail. It may mean that we come to the end of ourselves, or slow down and get quiet, before we realize that.

Once Elijah learned this lesson, he never again found himself in such a miserable condition. In fact, the latter part of his ministry was even greater than the first. He took up the prophets' school that Samuel had started and made three schools. He even finished in a blaze of glory—on a flaming chariot, horses and all (see 2 Kin. 2:11).

Are you feeling near burnout? Or have you passed burnout and now you're sitting there in a smoulder?

Take the advice God gave to a mighty prophet on one of the worst days of his life: Take a break, rest, and get good nourishment; see to your physical needs. Then be willing to put aside all your abilities, because they may be the very cause of your problems! Seek God in quietness.

Isn't it wonderful? By His word God made the heavens and earth and hung the stars in place. By His word He created every plant and animal—and even mankind. And His word still comes to you and me today. It's an inexhaustible source of power and vigor and creativity.

Maybe God's word to you today is this: Set aside all the gifts I've given you and seek Me again in the stillness of your heart.

David also learned that lesson. Like him, you can be renewed with a warrior's might. You, too, can say, the Lord "leads me beside quiet waters, he restores my soul" (Ps. 23:2-3).

Don't burn out. Shine for God every day! ✒

SIX

Habakkuk: Answers From God's Silence

All right, so these interesting men and women encountered the word of God during Old Testament days. Summing up what we've learned so far, what do their lives say to you and me today?

Hagar learned that, even in the worst situation of her life, God had a higher plan. Her response to God's word demonstrated that you and I also need to get a hold of God's vision for our lives—and accept it!

Esther discovered that, for us to enter into God's

plan, spiritual impurities of doubt, unbelief and fear need to be cleansed from our lives. Often that means going through fiery trials so that the gold He's placed within us can be revealed, as God's best work is done through purified vessels.

Eli's response to the word of God was a warning to us, showing the destructive forces we are open to if we *don't* heed God's word.

Through Elijah, we saw what happens if we set out to do good work—even God's work—in our own strength. Without the empowering of the Spirit, we'll crash and all our efforts may come to ruin. God wants us to enter into His plan, in His way, with His power.

So now you think you're ready to charge out and win great victories for God, right?

Not so fast! There is one great obstacle to being an overcomer that lies hidden in the path of almost every believer. Oh, you can make a brilliant start in this "faith race" we're all running. But if this one thing trips you up, what a tragedy!

Maybe you'll remember a tragic race that occurred during the summer Olympics several years ago. A woman named Mary Decker, a tremendously fast and natural runner, was a member of the U.S. track team. One of her toughest opponents was Zola Budd, from South Africa, known not only for her speed but also because she always ran barefoot.

When the starting gun sounded, Mary Decker took off like a jack rabbit. Her stride and form were beautiful to watch. You could almost feel the power pumping through her limbs as she flew around the track. Hot on her heels was Zola Budd.

Then it happened! Zola suddenly increased her kick, caught up with Mary and tried to slide into her lane. Possibly Mary shot a sideways glance to check out her opponent. I never heard for sure. Whatever the case, Mary stumbled over Zola's lanky stride—and fell.

I'll never forget the look of anguish on that young woman's face. Teammates ran out to help her get up. But she had no real physical injuries. The pain in her eyes came from the agony in her spirit. Because of one small trip, Mary Decker's race was lost!

By now I'm sure you're wondering what on earth I'm leading up to. What is the hidden obstacle that trips up so many Christians?

It's anger. Specifically, anger at God.

As I said, you can start out the race of faith with a strong stride. But I can almost guarantee that at some point in your Christian life you will run into circumstances that tempt you to get angry at God.

Some of you may be shocked. "Not me!" you say. "I'd never get mad at God." I warn you, in the words of Paul: "If you think you are standing firm, be careful that you don't fall!" (1 Cor. 10:12).

Others have a frighteningly nonchalant attitude about the whole thing. "Oh yeah," I've heard Christians say. "I'm really mad at God. In fact, I told *Him* a thing or two just this morning. Now I'm not speaking to Him until He straightens things out!" 👆

These folks think they're just like Job, who boldly questioned God. But the Bible says that, in all Job's heartbroken questioning, he "never sinned by charging God with wrongdoing" (Job 1:22). Job never showed disrespect for God by foolishly charging Him with wrongdoing or addressing Him with a bad attitude.

I want you to know that there are likely to be many times when you want to get real mad at God.

I've known of too many well-to-do Christian businessmen whose businesses were booming one day—and almost overnight they wound up in bankruptcy court.

Christian parents are not exempt from getting the midnight phone call, telling them their child is in jail for committing some serious crime.

God has promised us divine health and protection. And I personally cling to those promises every day! But we still keep hearing reports about believers stricken with cancer or some crippling disease. Time and again, we hear the heartwrenching stories about small children killed by drunk drivers or even by unwitting negligence on the part of loving parents.

One of the most heartbreaking stories I've ever heard was about a two-year-old and a Christmas Eve tragedy: The girl's mother kissed the child good-night and tucked her in her crib. Then she went up into the attic to get down the hidden presents.

But the tiny child climbed out of her crib almost as

soon as her mother left the room. When she couldn't find her mommy, she pulled open the front door and stepped outside into the freezing night.

Perhaps the wind blew the door shut. No one knows for sure. The young mother happily returned with all her brightly wrapped presents, placed them under the tree and went to bed.

It was daylight before anyone found the little girl out in the snow on the front porch. She was curled up, as if asleep. No one had heard her final cries for help.

Even if you've never personally suffered the kind of agony that poor mother must have felt, stories like this do have an effect on you, don't they? They stir something inside. They make you ask: Where was God when this terrible thing happened?

I know that I've heard countless other stories about miraculous healings, provisions, rescues. Countless stories that began like the story of this tiny tot but ended with a miracle. I've experienced miracles myself.

But I've also learned one thing: When the worst tragedy strikes, the wrong response is to get mad at God.

Nonetheless, God is a gracious Father. And He can stand up to our anger. In fact, sometimes, the moment hard circumstances expose our true, angry feelings, the word of God will come to us.

If anyone faced circumstances that would tempt one to be angry at God, it was the prophet Habakkuk.

Habakkuk lived about one hundred years before Esther, in about 620 B.C. (which confuses some people, because his short book is placed so much later than Esther's in the Old Testament). Israel was well past its golden age, which had come under David and Solomon. Israel in Habakkuk's time was like a rose, way past its prime, wilted and worm-shot.

The long-term effects of evil rulers such as Ahab, Jezebel and the sad list of national leaders that fills out 1 and 2 Kings had worn Israel down spiritually. Its spiritual walls of defense were in ruins. Because of that, its physical walls of stone were being torn down by foreign armies.

By Habakkuk's day, the rich no longer had any concern for the welfare of the poor. They ignored the laws God had given to Moses, which had built something of a social welfare system to provide for the poor, widows and orphans. In fact, the rich preyed upon the weak! They made their money by foreclosing on widows, demanding high prices from the helpless and accepting bribes from other rich men so they could win their lawsuits with the less fortunate.

Once the jewel among nations, the home of the presence of the Lord, the apple of God's eye—what a miserable, wretched place Israel had become!

Habakkuk loved God and hated sin. He hated what he saw happening among God's chosen people. He hated it so much that he had a hard time understanding why God didn't do something to stop it. Actually, he was getting downright bugged at God!

Listen to his opening complaint: "How long, O Lord, must I call for help, but you do not listen? Or cry out to you, 'Violence!' but you do not save?" (Hab. 1:2).

In other words, "What's the big idea, God? Here I am, crying out to You. I can see what's wrong here. Righteousness and justice are being perverted, and You aren't doing a blessed thing to stop it!"

Do you hear His frustration and anger?

It surely sounds familiar, doesn't it? So often we're tempted to think: Why are You doing this, God? This is terrible. And if You're not doing it, then why are You allowing it? You're sovereign; You're in charge, so either way it's all Your doing!

Habakkuk was angry at God for not doing something to stop the injustice and plain meanness he saw all around him. He was angry at God for not answering his prayers.

Boy, does that sound familiar!

It's the anger of the daddy we read about in chapter 4, the one who nearly turned against God when his little boy was suffering with asthma.

It's the anger of the young wife who prays boldly and faithfully for her husband to come to Christ—only to discover that he's divorcing her.

It's the anger of the businessman who seeks God's provision for his struggling business. But then things bottom-out financially.

Why aren't You listening, God? This is the angry

question that poured out of Habakkuk's spirit. But he was in for a double take when God finally did reply and sent His word.

God basically said, "You think I haven't been watching what's going on? You think I'm deaf and blind? Or that I don't care? You're wrong, Habakkuk!

"Even though you haven't been aware of what I'm up to, I've been working on a secret plan. What I've had in mind—well, you wouldn't have believed it, even if someone had told you" (see Hab. 1:5).

God does confide in us—sometimes. He does promise us wisdom and insight when we pray (see James 1:5). He does give us supernatural words of wisdom and knowledge (see 1 Cor. 12:8). But nowhere in Scripture does God promise to let us in on all His secrets and plans. He doesn't let us in on all His confidences.

That's where some of us make our first, big mistake when it comes to seeking the mind of God on a given matter. We think that God will always tell us everything. Even from an earthly viewpoint, that doesn't make sense.

Every army private in the trenches knows there are top-secret plans and missions afoot that his generals are not obligated to let him in on. He may shake his head sometimes, but he'll salute and obey orders if he's smart! Every American is aware that our government sometimes enters into private talks with foreign diplomats long before our news media sniffs them out.

The corporate employee knows that the chief executive officer is not obliged to consult him or her about a planned merger, a cut-back or expansion.

When you look at it that way, doesn't something seem wrong with the way we often demand that God answer our prayers our way, according to our dictates and our time schedule? Why is it that we often insist that God let us in on all His plans before we'll place our full trust in Him?

God told Habakkuk, "I've been getting a plan shaped up. The Chaldeans (or Babylonians) are going to swoop down upon Israel. They'll fall upon you like vultures. Like a hot, desert wind. Don't worry, they'll sweep out all the corruption you've been worried about!" (see Hab. 1:6-11).

Now it's a bit humorous what Habakkuk said next; it sounds so much like you and me. God had finally answered his plea; He'd whispered His plan in Habakkuk's ear. And what did the prophet say?

"Oh no, Lord!" Habakkuk cried. "What kind of a plan is that?"

Habakkuk objects, saying, "Look, aren't You the great and mighty God who is alive from everlasting? Aren't You eternally wise? Can't You come up with a better plan than this?

"Besides that, I thought You were holy and pure? How can You tolerate evil? How can You use an evil nation to bring about Your holy plan? I don't understand!" (See Hab. 1:12-17.)

THE BIBLE CAN CHANGE YOU

Do you hear your own complaint in Habakkuk's prayer? I've caught myself whining at God sometimes, saying, "OK, maybe You've got to change things, shake things up. But why do You have to do it this way?"

Now I believe God allows us to question Him. But we have to be on guard that we don't take the next step beyond questioning, which is rejecting God's wisdom and authority. That is rebellion against God's sovereign right to govern, and rebellion is as the sin of witchcraft (see 1 Sam. 15:23).

That seems a pretty harsh thing to say in this day and age, doesn't it? Maybe that's because we've swung so far over to the position where we allow ourselves to question everything authority says. It's true— we've seen a lot of corruption among authorities. But we can't allow our skepticism about earthly leaders—whom we should be praying for, whatever the case (see 1 Tim. 2:1-2)—to distort our view of God.

When we charge God with the same character flaws and weaknesses as human authorities, do you know whose side we're on? That's right—the side of Satan, God's adversary and accuser. I don't know about you, but I have no intention of getting on board his train, because I know where it's headed: for the pit!

It's important to understand what Habakkuk wound up saying to God at the end of the second prayer recorded in his book. He started by spilling out a typically human complaint: "Why are You doing it that way, Lord?" But he ended on a different note.

Maybe Habakkuk finally got an earful of his own wrong attitude. Look at the very end of his prayer. It's as if he's saying, "On the other hand, Lord, maybe I've been a sideline umpire. Maybe I don't see the big picture of this." So he says,

> I will stand at my watch and station myself on the ramparts, I will look to see what [the Lord] will say to me (Hab. 2:1).

In short, despite his human complaints, Habakkuk's heart was not closed to the Lord. He hadn't judged the Lord and hardened his heart toward Him. He was pliable and willing to be convinced of God's plan.

That's the attitude God is looking for in your heart and mine before He'll reveal even a glimpse of His higher purposes to us.

There are two main revelations God gave to Habakkuk as a result of his heart attitude.

The first revelation was that He was not bringing the evil upon Israel. God is not the author of evil. Then who is?

We know that Satan is the father of all lies (see John 8:44) and the one who seeks to devour you and me (see 1 Pet. 5:8). He causes all kinds of confusion.

But do you know what? It's also true that we can break down our own spiritual walls of protection and allow Satan a foothold in our lives, because of things like anger that we allow to fester (see Eph. 4:27).

God said to Habakkuk, "Your own people have plotted the ruin of innocent ones. They have shamed

their own house and brought ruin upon themselves"
(see Hab. 2:10).

A word of caution: You and I have to be careful not
to judge brothers and sisters who fall on hard times.
We have to be careful that we don't become like the
people of Jesus' day, who dragged the man born blind
before Him and demanded to know, "Who sinned, this
man or his parents?" (John 9:2).

For reasons unknown to us, God may allow an evil
situation to arise and stand for a time. But, as He revealed to the prophet Isaiah, He can be creative even
with evil (see Is. 45:7)! He can wrench Satan's worst
plot out of his hand and, using it like a sculptor's tool,
create good with it. In the end, if we hang on long
enough, we can say with Joseph, "What you meant
for evil, God turned to good!" (see Gen. 50:20).

As God said to Habakkuk, "Stop fretting and whining and complaining about Me. Stop accusing Me of
evil, when everything I have in mind is good. I'm in
My holy temple, so let all the earth be silent!" (see Hab.
2:20).

But what about those things that just seem too evil
to be of any good?

What about the deaths, divorces, the losses that can
never be repaired or replaced in this lifetime? As I said,
God may give us a glimpse of His higher plan—or He
may not. What then?

God had a second revelation for Habakkuk.

"Even if I don't reveal all My ways to you now,"

He said, "one day the whole earth will be filled with the knowledge of the glory of the Lord, as the waters cover the sea" (see Hab. 2:14).

God's reply to Habakkuk was a lot like what He said to the apostle Paul much later. Paul sought the Lord three times, asking Him to remove a "thorn" from his flesh. God did not remove that thorn. Instead, He said, "My grace is enough for you, Paul" (see 2 Cor. 12:9).

Personally, I believe in a God of miracles! I believe that we give up far too quickly, when God wants us to hang on no matter how bumpy the ride. We throw in the towel, sometimes just before His miraculous answer is about to come through. I will never stop encouraging men and women to believe God for a miracle!

But if God's answer is long in coming, there is one thing we must learn to do. God said, "My deliverance for Israel will come, Habakkuk. But it's a long way off as far as your lifetime goes." Habakkuk may not have understood, but he did something wonderful.

When the word of the Lord came to Habakkuk, he embraced it. In fact, his name means "embraced." He hugged the word of the Lord to his heart and never let go of it.

The result was that peace and joy flooded into him, washing away the complaints and gloom. He got so happy he sang! The whole last chapter of his book is a song. Not only that, he gives instructions to directors of music on how this song is to be sung. He said,

"Call the worship singers together. Get out the stringed instruments. Strike up the band! God is still God, and we're all going to sing about it" (see Hab. 3).

Maybe you're in the midst of a spiritually dark time. Maybe you can't see what good can ever come out of the situation you're in. Perhaps you're thinking: Come on, Marilyn. Sing? You're going to tell me to sing? You've gotta' come up with something better than that!

Yes, there is something better. Look at what Habakkuk sang about: "Lord, I have heard of your fame; I stand in awe of your deeds" (Hab. 3:2).

Habakkuk looked back over all the history of the Israelites, and he drew on all that God had done. The promise to Abraham. The salvation of Noah and his family. Deliverance from Pharaoh, the parting of the Red Sea, the miracles of manna from heaven and quail. Victory over the Philistines and Amorites and Ammonites....

Let me ask you: How many times have you been in the midst of trouble, and it seems as if God has never done anything for you ever before? How often are we tempted to forget the love and miracles God showered on us yesterday and turn back to complaining against Him?

Personally, I went through just such a time.

For many years after I became a Christian, we prayed for the salvation of my father. He was a good man and a good daddy. But Mom and Wally and I prayed for years for Daddy to open his heart to the Lord. Sometimes we could tell God was at work, and other times it just seemed as if nothing was happening.

Finally, when Daddy was in his late sixties, he gave his life to the Lord! It wasn't just a quiet, inner thing that you had to pry out of him. Daddy openly loved the Lord and served Him. I was ecstatic! Our miracle had come through.

But just as suddenly, only six months later, Daddy died. I was devastated.

Just like Habakkuk, I found myself weeping, crying out to God, saying, "This isn't fair, God! Just when I could get to know my father in a deeper, spiritual relationship in Christ. Just when things were turning around in his life. Why did You do it this way?"

That's how I found myself crying out to God on my bed the night Daddy died. The darkness around me seemed so deep and black. How could there be any good in this?

But then something wonderful happened.

There in the dark, as my heart cried out for comfort, I suddenly felt a wonderful presence. It started as a sense of well being, then slowly grew until I was surrounded with a blanket of love and comfort.

Then I knew. I no longer had my earthly daddy. But my heavenly Daddy was all around me. Even in the dark. Even when it looked bad. He would never leave me. Even though I couldn't see the plan, He had everything in control.

It was as if the picture was suddenly reversed. I'd been focusing only on death and loss and pain. I could now focus on Dad's salvation, the fact that he was standing before God right at that moment, seeing his Savior and Lord face-to-face. I even got a little envious!

That got me thinking about the miracle of our salvation. The incredible love God poured out on us when He sent Jesus to shed His blood. I thought about the words of Paul:

> Who shall separate us from the love of Christ? Shall trouble or hardship or persecution or famine or nakedness or danger or sword?...No! In all these things we are more than conquerors through him who loved us (Rom. 8:35,37).

Surrounding the mystery of my father's death—wrapping it not in shrouds of loss but in the white robes of victory—was the love of Christ. Because of Jesus' victory over sin and death, Daddy was with God! And the silent sense of God's presence with me in spirit was stronger proof of His love for me, perhaps, than if He had given me some answer to satisfy my mind.

At Daddy's funeral, I did weep—but they were tears of joy. Just like Habakkuk, I couldn't help recounting all of God's love. Even death couldn't stop me from singing!

Anger at God is the reason a lot of Christians fail to finish the race. The reason they turn from Him just before the victory comes. But it doesn't have to be that way. You don't have to lose!

God's word to Habakkuk was twofold: Trust My higher plan, even though I can't show it to you now. And one day it will all be revealed to you; you will have full knowledge of all My glorious dealings, as the waters cover the sea.

When God's word to you is not "Let Me show you" but "Wait," then trust Him! Choose to stand on the side of the heavenly witnesses, who are singing the song of Moses and the Lamb: "Just and true are your ways, King of the ages" (Rev. 15:3).

When you pick up the song of praise and victory, Satan cannot confuse you. No matter what lies he's whispering in your ears about God, don't go down his side road smack into a snare. Don't believe him for a minute!

"God is light; in him there is no darkness at all" (1 John 1:5).

Make that your victory cry, and you will see spiritual confusion evaporate like fog on a sunny morning. Like Habakkuk, stand on the side of God. Let your heart sing a new song!

Soon you'll be watching in awe as God's bright, new pathway opens before your eyes.

SEVEN

Ruth: Part of the Curse or Part of the Blessing

S ometimes it amazes me how much of our time we spend thinking, worrying and praying about ourselves. Don't misunderstand me. I have no doubt that God wants us to come to Him with all our personal hurts, questions, requests and needs. He hears every prayer of His children.

But there's a bigger picture we need to get hold of if we want to get on with our spiritual journey.

Through the early chapters, we've seen how God wants to work in us. Or you could say He's working on us. He works to make us sensitive to His word. He cleans us up and cleans us out—even the dark, hidden corners of our spirit—so He can use us as His vessels.

It's comforting to me that God isn't like the corporate executive who's unconcerned about his employees—one who's interested only in the "bottom line." And He isn't like the average, modern consumer, either. By that I mean He doesn't use us, like a paper cup or a disposable plastic fork, and then toss us aside. When He's through, what was wood, hay and stubble in us has been changed to gold. A gold cup, full of light!

But God does have purposes. Big ones! He does have a bottom line, so to speak.

One of the big purposes God has for you is to make you a blessing for others. He wants to involve you in His ultimate goal of reaching out to the lost. By His word, He wants to transform the inner you so that He can reach out through you to His other lost and hurting sheep.

I believe there's been a big misunderstanding about the concept of blessing. Because the church for so long taught that God was angry, jealous and vengeful, it's taken quite a bit just to convince most Christians that God is *not* mad at them. He wants to bless you, prosper you and make you healthy, because He loves to give good and perfect gifts to His children (see James 1:17).

However, He also gives us gifts that He doesn't want us to hoard just for ourselves. As far as finances go, God needs to speak to you personally about your love offerings. But there is one gift that I can say for certain God wants you to spread around. That is the free gift of abundant life that His Spirit pours into you.

God's personal word to you says: I want to involve you in My great and wonderful plan of salvation. Think of it! Isn't that amazing?

You see, we're all like travelers on our way to an eternally significant rendezvous with God.

Unfortunately, for lots and lots of people—some of them friends, neighbors, co-workers and relatives you care about—the meeting isn't going to be so happy. It might be very, very tragic.

For others, even some Christians, the face-to-face meeting with God might not be tragic—they will get into their eternal mansion—but the meeting will still be sad. Maybe they allowed circumstances to wear down their faith. They limped through life, always weighed down, never an overcomer. They never came close to doing all that God had in mind for their lives.

That's where you and I come into the picture. Just look at this great image, from Psalm 84: "Blessed are those whose strength is in you, who have set their hearts on pilgrimage. As they pass through the Valley of Baca, they make it a place of springs....They go from strength to strength till each appears before God in Zion" (vv. 5-7).

You need to know that the Valley of Baca is a legendary place, a terrible, desolate place on the way to Jerusalem. Pilgrims had to pass through this miserable gully—or at least see and smell it—on their way to worship. No one knows for sure, but it might have been the Valley of Hinnom, outside the city gates, a smoldering ravine full of dung and refuse that was known as *gehenna*, which became the Jewish symbol for hell. But look at what this psalm says!

When you and I who are growing in Christ pass through a desolate place, what are we to do about it? We draw our strength from Him and we "make it a place of springs"! We are to let the life-giving "water" of the Holy Spirit flow through us. Why? Just so we can enjoy His refreshing life in us?

No! We are called to bring a refreshing drink to the desolate, thirsty and stumbling people all around us. Some are on their way to *gehenna*. Some are miserable and staggering on their way up to Jerusalem to worship.

Sometimes I think we've really lost sight of God's plan of salvation. I think we're also confused about His plan for helping His children grow spiritually. We leave everything up to Him. But that was never God's plan.

From the moment Adam and Eve brought the curse upon mankind, God's plan of salvation involved us. He didn't say to Adam and Eve, "OK, you blew it big. So get out of My way." He promised that salvation from the curse would come through the seed of Eve (see Gen. 3:15).

Now you may be saying: Sure, God can use some

people. But how can He use someone like me? I'm far from perfect. Sometimes I don't even feel much like a child of God. How can God want to use me to lead anyone closer to Him?

There was one person in the Bible who must have felt exactly the same way—a woman who would have thought those same thoughts, had she known the role God had in mind for her.

But the word of God had come to her.

Her name was Ruth.

The book of Ruth is little, one of the smallest in the Bible. But it's like a central pillar in revealing God's plan of salvation.

The Jews read the book of Ruth every year on the feast of Pentecost, during which they traditionally wave two loaves of bread before God. That action symbolizes both the Jew and the Gentile joining in God's feast of promises. Don't you think it's pretty interesting that the way was opened for us Gentiles to come into fellowship with God again when the Holy Spirit fell on the day of Pentecost? (See Acts 2.)

When the book opens, we find two women—Ruth and Naomi—right in the middle of a miserable, cursed situation.

You see, Naomi's husband, Elimelech, had moved his family out of Israel during a time of famine. *Elimelech* means "God of the king" or "God is King," but he certainly didn't act as if God were his king. He trusted in the protection of the false god of Moab—

a deity named Chemosh (see 1 Kin. 11:7).

God Himself had such loathing for the land of Moab that, once, in a prophecy, He said, "Let Moab wallow in her vomit" (Jer. 48:26).

The move to Moab didn't do much for Elimelech's family. In fact, Elimelech died there. And his two sons married heathen, Moabite women, which was expressly forbidden by the Lord. Then those sons died, leaving Naomi a widow in a foreign land surrounded by enemies of her God.

Now the stage is set for you to meet Ruth. And the stage is set for Ruth to meet the word of the Lord!

As Naomi prepared to return to Israel, she begged her daughters-in-law to stay behind in Moab. "Find yourselves husbands here. Settle down. Start a new life for yourselves."

Her next words are key: "It is more bitter for me than for you, because the Lord's hand has gone out against me" (Ruth 1:13). And she said, "The Lord has afflicted me; the Almighty has brought misfortune upon me" (v. 21).

Naomi felt deserted by the Lord. She was in a cursed place, separated from God. Her husband and sons— all that she loved—had been stripped from her. Her conclusion was that God had judged her and cast her away from His presence. She felt the bitter lostness of hell in her soul.

Put yourself in Ruth's position.

Something in her soul recoiled from Naomi's words.

106

Whether she had heard from her Hebrew husband, Naomi's son, about the God of Israel—the great God of mercy, who is slow to anger and quick to forgive—we can't say.

We can say that, as Ruth looked upon Naomi in her hell of misery and destitution, she felt something stir in her spirit. And she heard one word: love.

But all around her lay her own land. Her own people. All that was familiar.

In that moment Ruth had to choose. We know that the other daughter-in-law, Orpah, quickly took Naomi up on the offer. She hugged her mother-in-law around the neck, turned and hightailed it for home. But Ruth had heard the word. More than that, the word was in her, changing her.

And so we hear her famous reply. Words of compassion and self-sacrifice that are so heartstirring that we use them in wedding ceremonies as men and women pledge their lives to each other: "Don't urge me to leave you....Where you go I will go....Your people will be my people and your God my God....May the Lord deal with me, be it ever so severely, if anything but death separates you and me" (vv. 16-17).

Ruth knew Naomi was lost, poor, without hope. But she allowed her heart to be transformed by God's word: love! And so she could see this woman through His eyes of compassion and mercy. Ruth was even willing to condemn herself to living under the judgment of God that seemed to rest on Naomi, if that's what it took, to show Naomi the kind of love that was in her heart.

No wonder God chose Ruth. No wonder her life became an important thread in the wonderful plan He had been weaving down through the ages.

Frankly, to me, the whole Bible is mainly about God's plan to reverse the curse. It's about God, working out a plan that will bring the most lost, wretched soul back into full fellowship with Himself—with His nature and power alive in us.

What better way to illustrate that plan than to take a Moabite woman and bring her into the story of redemption?

Once I understood where Ruth had come from and God's complete disgust with her god and her people, I no longer doubted that God could transform anybody or that He could use anybody in bringing others closer to Himself.

The story of Ruth gets better the further you go. In the second chapter, we see Ruth as an alien in the promised land. But was she an outcast?

No. Ruth was allowed to glean in the fields of her kinsman Boaz. You see, the law of God through Moses said that a tenth of all the crops had to be left standing in the fields, unharvested. This was so the poor and even the foreigners, who had no land of their own on which to raise crops, could harvest something.

This is a beautiful picture of God's offering of grace and mercy to you and me—if we'll reach out our hands and take it. This is an important point I don't want you to miss.

Some Christians, in their secret heart, don't get at all excited about winning their neighbors to Christ. The idea of spiritual fellowship in which they encourage other Christians doesn't really do much to rouse them either. Maybe you feel that way sometimes. But why?

I believe it's because some of us aren't experiencing the abundant life Jesus promised (see John 10:10). Those "rivers of living water" He also promised can sometimes feel as if they've hit the summer drought!

There are a number of reasons why the "abundant Christian life" can grow dull and lifeless. But one of the main reasons we lose our zeal is guilt.

Take a moment to think about it: Are you gleaning God's grace and mercy every day, or are you living on a harvest of guilt? Are you still browbeating yourself for the way you let God down last year? A month ago? Yesterday? Just this morning?

It seems to me that those guilt-producing failures always happen just when you're about to be used by God.

For example, how many Sunday mornings do you wake up with every expectation of having a pleasant breakfast with the family, followed by a leisurely drive to church. You can't wait to get there and praise the Lord!

Then, at the breakfast table, one child dumps over his orange juice—right in the lap of child number two.

Child number two shouts, "You idiot!"

World War III follows.

After more commotion, you've reached your boiling point. You're now fifteen minutes late getting on the road to church—just like last week and the week before. And you hear yourself shout angrily, "Get in the car! Right now, or I'll knock you cross-eyed! We're going to church to praise the Lord!"

Some witness to your kids, right? Not to mention your spouse (and the neighbors, if your windows were open). By the time you finally settle into that pew I know what you're thinking: Boy, what a rotten Christian I am. I don't have any right to praise the Lord. He doesn't want to hear from me now.

Or how about experiences like these:

Something at the office sets you off. You lose your cool. Someone mutters under her breath, "And I thought you were a Christian." You slink away and vow never to open your mouth about Jesus Christ again.

New neighbors move in across the street. You really intend to bake a cake, or at least invite your new neighbors in for coffee. But you get busy, running the kids to music lessons and sports practices. Then you come down with the flu—and who shows up at your front door with a tray of homemade cookies? All you can think is: How can I tell her about God's love, when I've been such a lousy example of His kindness?

The list could get pretty long. After you're a

Christian, you're bound to meet the old friend you used to gossip with. The friend whose off-color jokes used to make you double up with laughter. The old drinking buddies, or even the guy you used to sell dope to.

Are you saying to yourself: What good am I to God? How can I open my mouth to speak for Him—or serve others in His name—after my failures? Or are you telling yourself: I'm just not a good enough Christian to encourage anyone else?

Stop sowing thorns and weeds in your spirit! Once you confess your failures to God, let 'em go! Start harvesting God's mercy toward you.

Take a page out of Ruth's notebook. Naomi learned that Ruth had been gleaning in the fields of Boaz, her kinsman. He had shown great mercy to Ruth, telling his men not to bother her and even to leave extra grain so her work would be easier. Ruth took advantage of that goodness, and it pleased Boaz. Naomi knew that Ruth had found favor with Boaz.

So she presented Ruth with a plan, and Ruth bought it right away. She probably did not understand the plan, but she did everything just as her mother-in-law told her.

Ruth washed and splashed on the latest cologne. She put on her most attractive outfit. Then she went down to the threshing floor where Boaz was winnowing barley. She waited till he had finished a hard day's work, eaten his evening meal and lain down to sleep.

Then Ruth did something that seems very strange to modern, Western Christians.

Once Boaz was asleep, she went over and lifted up the outer cloak with which he'd covered his feet. Then she lay down and covered herself with it.

What a beautiful picture God has given us in His word! You see, in the ancient Hebrew marriage ceremony, the groom took his best robe and put it around his bride. It symbolized the rejoining of the woman (the rib!) into the side of the man. And he said, "No one may hurt her. I am her protector now!"

Jesus is our Protector—yours and mine. He is the one who purchased your complete forgiveness with His blood. So when He places His robe of righteousness around your shoulders, He's only doing what He's always wanted to do as your heavenly Bridegroom. He's saying to one and all, "This is My beloved—protected from the claims of all others. No one can lay a charge against this one. My righteousness covers all!"

Isn't this exactly what Paul wrote? "Who will bring any charge against those whom God has chosen? It is God who justifies. Who is he that condemns?" (Rom. 8:33).

Who brings charges against us? Who is he who condemns? Good question! I think I've figured it out. How about you?

It's Satan. Doesn't it make a lot of sense to you, considering Satan is totally pitted against the purpose of

God? God wants to reconcile the whole world to Himself (see 2 Cor. 5:19), and He wants to win the world through you and me (see Matt. 28:16-20). So it's logical that Satan wants to wipe you out—make you completely powerless and ineffective.

What better way to do it than with a preemptive strike? Satan will constantly throw in your face everything you've done wrong from the time you were three years old to the latest tiff with your spouse or the last time you got frustrated and kicked the dog.

But Jesus has wrapped His protective robe around your shoulders, and Satan cannot come around laying any charges on you without first having to face Him! And He has already satisfied Satan's legal claim to you.

Again, the book of Ruth gives us a tender picture of the way Jesus redeemed us—"bought back" Satan's claim to us.

When Boaz awoke to find Ruth lying at his feet, I'll bet he broke into a big grin. He knew exactly what this young woman was up to. She was proposing to him! He knew she had real, noble character to do what she'd done (see Ruth 3:11). Those first stirrings he'd felt when he saw her gleaning in the fields burst into all-out love.

"I want to marry you," he told her, "but there's a big problem I have to solve first. A legal matter. There's another relative in town who's closer to Naomi's family. Technically, he has claim to you first. But I'll go talk to him, and I vow that I'll redeem you for my own" (see Ruth 3:12-13).

So Boaz went to the other kinsman before all the elders of the city and presented his case. The kinsman agreed to give Boaz the right to marry Ruth. As a sign of the transaction, the man gave Boaz his shoe.

Now the shoe was a symbol of legal claim to a piece of property. It may have come from God's word to Joshua: "I will give you every place where you set your foot" (Josh. 1:3). Giving someone your shoe in a property transaction was like saying, "I no longer have any right to set foot here. The property is now yours."

So when Jesus purchased your salvation and mine, He bought all property rights! Satan no longer has any business slipping one measly little toe in your life. In fact, you have the right to put your foot down any time he tries to accuse you. You can crush his head! (See Luke 10:19.)

In the end, Ruth became the bride of Boaz—just as you and I have become the bride of our Kinsman-Redeemer, Jesus.

But imagine this scenario: Just as the rabbi had been about to pronounce the couple husband and wife, Ruth had interrupted: "Hold on. You all seem to have missed something here. There's Moabite blood in these veins. I came from that yucky place where they worship a false deity. My people are enemies of Israel."

But that's not what happened. Ruth had let go of the past. And if anyone ever dared to whisper, as she walked past on the way to the village well, "Here comes that Moabitess. She has no right coming here," the words sloughed off her back. Boaz had wrapped his robe of protection around her. He had redeemed her as his own. No whispered accusation or threat could stop her from drawing water.

And nothing should stop you from drawing water from the wells of salvation, or from pouring it out on others who are thirsty or dying.

God used Ruth in His plan to bring salvation to the whole world. You see, Boaz and Ruth had a son named Obed, which means "servant of God" or "worshipper of God." His son was Jesse, whose son was David, who became king of Israel. And, of course, King David was the ancestor of Jesus, the long-awaited Messiah of Israel and Savior of the world.

And God called a despised, cursed Moabite woman to take part in that salvation. We even find Ruth's name listed in the genealogy of Jesus found in Matthew 1.

What are the weeds of guilt that you've been harvesting? Isn't it time to uproot them and let them be burned up in God's cleansing flames of love and forgiveness?

You want to let the Holy Spirit flow through you, don't you? Well, that's exactly what He wants! So you're right on track.

I know a big, gentle man named Dave who lives here in Colorado. Guilt nearly kept him from one of the most important spiritual breakthroughs of his life.

As a teenager, Dave was a complete rebel. His dad

had deserted the family, and Dave had a pretty rough upbringing. He joined the service but got himself drummed out. He was involved with a wild crowd, which led to drug use and robbery. Soon he landed in jail.

Dave came to the Lord, and when he was released from prison, he went straight and got married. Eventually, the Lord sent him back to prison—as a chaplain. He went behind bars every day to tell men about the love and forgiveness and new life they could find in Jesus Christ. Because he had walked where they'd walked, the men listened to him.

Shortly after Dave started ministering in prison, tragedy struck.

He got a phone call late one night. His brother, who was working as a night security guard at a local business, had been shot by a hold-up man. He was dead.

But the heartwrenching part was this: The man who'd murdered Dave's brother had been taken to the prison where Dave worked!

The morning after the murder, Dave drove to the prison, his heart churning with anger and hatred. How could he face this man as his chaplain—this man who had murdered his own brother?

When Dave walked into the cell block, he could tell that the guards and prisoners had heard the terrible news. He felt as if every eye was on him as he silently made his way toward the new prisoner's cell. How was he going to treat the man? Even he couldn't answer that question.

Somehow, he got through the first, brief interview with the murderer—a tough, mean little guy with an arrogant disposition. He didn't even seem the least bit sorry!

Dave gave him a Bible. He never told the guy that he was the brother of the man he'd killed. He was determined to show the love of Christ.

As the days, weeks and months passed, he never felt a twinge of love for the man. As far as Dave knew, the guy didn't have an inkling of the connection between him and the dead security guard. And Dave had to fight against bitterness and growing hatred—and another feeling that was trying to swallow him: guilt.

"How can I face any of those men every day? How can I tell them that Christ will forgive any sin they've committed, when I feel the way I do? What business do I have being a prison chaplain?"

Instead of giving in to those accusing thoughts and quitting, Dave had an encounter with the word of God.

He knew what the Bible said: "Let us not become weary in doing good, for at the proper time we will reap a harvest if we do not give up" (Gal. 6:9).

He'd worked with some tough, unbending characters. But this prisoner—this situation—was off the scale!

Dave called out to Jesus in prayer again and again: "If it were up to me, I'd give up, Lord. I have nothing to give—no love, nothing. I don't know how I can keep ministering to this guy. But, if it's possible, Lord, let Your love come through in me.''

Almost a year went by, and one day the man with the chip on his shoulder asked to see Dave. When Dave sat down across from him, he was in for a big surprise.

Through the prison grapevine the prisoner had learned who Dave was.

"How can you treat me the way you do?" the man asked. "I killed your brother. But you've never shown me anything but kindness. I can't take it anymore."

Dave thought of all the things he wanted to say to this man. It took one more supreme effort—one more prayer shot silently to heaven—but Dave was able to open his mouth. And he spoke out for Christ.

That day a murderer heard about the love of God in a way that struck home with greater power than a thousand sermons.

But it never would have happened if Dave hadn't fought and overcome the monster of guilt.

I like to remind myself of a powerful truth that the wonderful, Dutch saint Corrie ten Boom discovered. After spending part of World War II in a Nazi prison camp, where her sister Betsy was beaten and finally died, some years later Corrie met one of their former guards.

She'd just preached about God's love to the downcast German people, and the man stood there smiling, his hand outstretched, waiting for Corrie to take it in a gesture of forgiveness.

But only hatred blazed in Corrie's heart. And a sense of terrible inadequacy. How could she be preaching love when she couldn't feel love?

Corrie could only pray silently: Lord Jesus, forgive me and help me to forgive this man.

Woodenly, she reached out her hand to the former guard.

But suddenly, as their fingers met, a wave of love ran through her body like a miracle.

"And so," Corrie wrote in her book *The Hiding Place*, "I discovered that it is not on our forgiveness any more than on our goodness that the world's healing hinges, but on His."

Everything we have is a gift. Love. Forgiveness. Fellowship with God. Righteousness.

If God tells us to share those gifts freely—even as He's making them more and more real in our own lives—what choice do we have?

You'll find real power by sharing God's gifts of salvation and spiritual encouragement when you know His love has changed you.

And even when you don't.

Like Boaz, Jesus is not about to let anyone lay claim to you. He purchased you, and you're His.

EIGHT

Ezra: Make Up Your *Heart* About God

I don't know about you, but it seems as if the challenges in my life don't ever quit. There's always something new to stretch my faith.

Every time I think it's finally all peaceful on one battle line, a new skirmish breaks out on another front. For instance, if Wally and I have just prayed through some question in our marriage and come to terms, then sure as shootin' a problem will come up with, say, one of our children. Or with the ministry. Or some kind of sickness tries to latch on. I thank God for the smooth times, but I'm always on guard against more fiery darts!

It takes a lot of faith just to withstand the almost constant onslaughts of the adversary, doesn't it? Not to mention the opposition we face when God calls us to do a work for Him. Sometimes it can even feel as if our best friends are working against us!

One person who had to face opposition on every front was a scribe whom we generally pay little attention to. Most Christians know of him because of the Bible book that bears his name, but they don't recognize that without him the written word of God might have been lost to us. If anyone can speak to you and me today about keeping our spirits right and our heads level when everything is coming unglued, it's this man—Ezra.

Ezra means "God is my helper"—and boy, was he ever going to need help!

Ezra, one of the Hebrew exiles living in Persia around 500 B.C., was to emerge as a hero, but in many ways Ezra was probably the last man anyone would have expected to show the courage he showed.

To get the impact of how God used Ezra, you've got to see this larger picture.

About one hundred years before Ezra's day, before the Israelites were swept into Babylonian captivity, Jeremiah had predicted the downfall of Israel. He'd warned them that God was going to clear out the land because of their idolatry and corruption.

Jeremiah had also warned the people that God would

even allow the Babylonians to destroy the magnificent temple Solomon had built. Why? Because the worship of the people had become polluted. They had brought idol worship into the temple. And in their national pride they had thought: We've got God's temple here—all the external evidence that God is with us—so we're doing OK.

But God was greatly grieved with their spiritual adultery.

So Jeremiah wept for the downfall of Israel, and he promised that, once God had made a clean sweep, He would bring His chosen ones back to the land and start all over. And He would do it in a miraculous way, by the hand of a heathen king.

In Ezra's day—perhaps when he was a boy or a young man—Jeremiah's prophecy was being fulfilled! Imagine the excitement when Cyrus, the Persian king, issued a special decree: "The God of heaven has called me to rebuild the temple in Jerusalem" (see Ezra 1:2).

Not only that, Cyrus financed the whole project. He also gave back all the gold and silver articles Nebuchadnezzar had swiped from God's temple when he had raided Jerusalem and overturned everything.

Surely the Spirit of God was moving! You can almost see the captive Israelites, running from house to house with the news: "This is it! God has heard our prayers and answered! He's going to restore the temple and the land and our former glory!"

National heroes arose, princes of the Hebrew people

who were led by Zerubbabel. They called out more than forty-two thousand Israelites, warriors and workers—plus thousands of servants and two hundred singers. They amassed thousands of camels, horses, mules and donkeys to carry the money and the glittering temple objects back to Israel. What a procession that must have been as they paraded out of Babylon. I can imagine throngs of Israelites standing along the roads to cheer them on their way.

But quietly, in the background, the word of the Lord came to a studious, serious young man named Ezra.

Ezra was a descendant of Aaron, and his family served in the priesthood with quiet dignity. Tradition says that his father wrote Psalm 119. Whether or not that's true, we do know that Ezra was captivated by its message about the law of God: "Blessed are they who keep [the Lord's] statutes and seek him with all their heart....I seek you with all my heart...I have hidden your word in my heart that I might not sin against you" (Ps. 119:2,10-11).

Ezra had a love affair going on with the word of God! He is one, tradition tells us, who preserved the word of God while Israel was in captivity. That meant committing the whole law of Moses to memory. It meant singing the psalms over and over so not a word would be lost. It meant painstaking hours of writing books of the prophets out by hand. Ezra is reputedly the man who assembled and arranged the Old Testament in the order we have it today.

But whom do Christians teach their children about? Whom do we most want to be like? Joshua, Gideon, Samson, David. All the tough guys! All the handsome, athletic hero-types. These men certainly did great things for God—but it was through Ezra, the ol' bookworm who hid God's word in his heart, that we know about the heroes at all.

Ezra's diligence and hard work really stir me up to study God's word. That's one of the most important foundation stones in spiritual growth: knowing the Bible.

There are so many other things that demand our attention, though. Television. Videos. Magazines. Books. Now I'm not saying you should throw out your TV and burn your books (unless you're watching or reading trash). But the truth is, so many Christians don't develop the kind of love affair with the Bible that Ezra did. And it takes a little bit of work.

If you're married, do you remember the first time you met the man or woman you eventually wed? For most people it's not "love at first sight." It takes time, getting to know someone, maybe even having a few struggles and tough times together to know you're in love. And if it wasn't work when you were dating, it surely is work after you're married to stay in love!

Why is it, then, that so many Christians think all the wisdom and beauty of the Bible just appear in your head from a few easy readings? Psalm 119 talks about studying God's word, meditating on it day and night, seeking and hungering for its light and wisdom. You can take that slogan athletes apply to their physical workout and apply it to Bible study: "No pain—no gain!"

Ezra was busy loving God's word. Because of that, God used him to bring about one of Israel's greatest revivals. But not before Ezra faced serious perils. ✿

Once the band of heroes got back to Jerusalem, some of the glory dulled a bit. The surrounding people put up a big fuss about having a temple rebuilt next door. They got up a huge petition to King Artaxerxes, the ruler who came along after Cyrus, demanding he call things to a halt.

"You know these Israelites have a reputation for being rebellious," the petitioners complained. "If you allow them to finish their temple, they'll overthrow your rule and make a big mess of things" (see Ezra 4).

Artaxerxes halted the building; then a few years later, a new ruler, King Darius, agreed to let the temple reconstruction continue. By then, however, the situation between the Israelites in Jerusalem and their neighbors was a little hot. Construction went on under fear of an attack; things were tense. Jerusalem, with its broken-down walls, was a place for stouthearted warriors, not quiet, bookish scholars.

And wouldn't you know it? That was the very moment the word of the Lord came to Ezra, sending him right into the middle of a hot and hostile situation.

King Darius (called Artaxerxes in Ezra 7:1) summoned Ezra one day. What a surprise it must have been. "Ezra," he said, "I hear that things are a bit rocky in Jerusalem, so I've got a big job for you. I'm commissioning you to go and get things in order."

Why did Artaxerxes choose Ezra? The king said it himself: "Because the law of God is in your hand" (see Ezra 7:14).

It was as if the king was saying, "You have such control and mastery of God's word that it's like a sword in your hand. Or like a scepter. I can see that you know how to rule over circumstances. That's why I've chosen you to go and set things right."

So he sent Ezra to do two things.

One was to re-establish the worship of God in the temple. You see, I think Artaxerxes was smart. He wanted to see a return on Persia's investment. The people had built this lavish temple, but it sounds as if it wasn't being used properly. Artaxerxes said, "Start the sacrifices again." Whether or not Artaxerxes was a true worshipper of God we don't know. At least he was a sharp landlord, and because Ezra knew the law of God he was chosen as property manager.

The second thing Artaxerxes commissioned Ezra to do was to act as his governor over Jerusalem. He was to set up a civil government, appointing judges and magistrates to rule the people according to God's laws. Once again, the king had called on Ezra, the one man who knew these laws so well that talking about them was like breathing.

Have you ever considered all the amazing promises Solomon related to us in the book of Proverbs? Over and over again, he tells us to dig into God's wisdom and His laws because of the tremendous benefits they will bring us—health, peace of mind and soul, prosperity, guidance in dark times, protection.

God's word doesn't just benefit us spiritually; it will prosper us in the natural, everyday world. If you learn godly principles—if you hide God's word in your heart—it will benefit you in the workplace, in the market. God's wisdom through you will be like a light to your co-workers and your neighbors. You and everyone around you will be blessed by its light!

So Ezra knew God's word—but he was no spiritual superman. Like every one of us, Ezra had a choice to make when the word of God came to him through Artaxerxes.

You see, the trip from Persia to Israel was not a pleasant one. There were no jets and no super-highways. There was just a treacherous, rugged road through bandit-infested mountains and blistering deserts. And it wasn't a one- or two-day jaunt, either. Getting to Jerusalem would take more than four months of hard travel (see Ezra 7:8-9).

Besides that, we read that "Ezra had devoted himself to the study and observance of the Law of the Lord, and to teaching its decrees and laws" (Ezra 7:10). Ezra probably enjoyed a pretty good measure of honor and respect from his people. He was the best-known, best-loved Bible teacher of his day! Naturally speaking, why would he want to leave all that praise and adulation to make a dangerous trip into the unknown?

Ezra did make the trip, though. He did it for the love of God and his love of the law of God. He did it because he had already settled it in his heart: God's word is law.

But the dangerous journey was not the greatest peril he had to face. Once he'd crossed the border into Israel, he probably thought, Whew! I made it. But his heart must have gone cold when he learned about the true, sorry state of things.

When Ezra was greeted by the leaders of the people at the borders of Israel, he noticed a funny thing. Even though word had gone before Ezra, saying that he was returning the temple articles, there were no Levites among his welcoming party. No priests had come out to rejoice with him.

So he sent for some priests, and a few came. (See Ezra 8:15-36.) Maybe they were a little subdued, I don't know. Finally, the whole crew traveled the rest of the way to Jerusalem. Once Ezra got there, he found out exactly why the priests weren't so happy about his coming.

Ezra discovered that a terrible thing had happened. Now keep in mind that the reason God swept these people out of the land was because of their spiritual adulteries. They had insisted on marrying heathen wives, which brought polluted practices into their homes and into the temple worship.

And now, the men who had returned to build God's temple anew had gone out and found heathen wives. Even the priests and Levites, who, of all people, should have known better!

When Ezra heard this news, he ripped his clothes, tore hair from his head and sat down in the dust to weep. He said, "I'm utterly appalled at what you've done" (see Ezra 9:3).

These great "heroes" had rebuilt a beautiful temple. But their heart-attitude was no different from that of their ancestors, the men who had gotten Israel in deep trouble in the first place. So as far as Ezra was concerned, they might as well have built a warehouse. Hadn't these guys learned anything?

But I wonder if there was another reason why Ezra tore his clothes and wept. He knew the history of Israel better than anyone there. And he knew how his people treated anyone who brought them a hard word. Jeremiah had been thrown in a stinking cistern. Other prophets had been stoned or cut in two. Because he knew the reputation of this city, he lamented just as Jesus would do hundreds of years later: "O Jerusalem, you who kill the prophets and stone those sent to you" (Matt. 23:37).

And now here was Ezra, sitting in the dirt, knowing that he was one of those sent to Jerusalem. In that instant, God's word to him was clear: Ezra's real mission was to preach repentance! He knew the law, and the law said those heathen wives had to go. And what man was going to be happy to hear that he had to get rid of his wife?•

But Ezra knew the first thing he had to do. He prayed. At the time of the evening sacrifice, he fell on his knees and cried out to God in a loud voice: "O my God, I am too ashamed and disgraced to lift up my face to you, my God, because our sins are higher than our heads....What can we say after this? For we have disregarded the commands you gave" (Ezra 9:6,10).

Wait a minute. Who should be ashamed? And who had disregarded God's commands?

Certainly not Ezra. Personally, he was the model of righteousness. He had soaked himself in God's laws. He wasn't one of those men with a heathen wife.

I love the life of Ezra, because it reveals one of the most powerful secrets about the word of God. God certainly has a place for His prophets, His teachers and preachers. But I believe God has a special place in His heart for His intercessors!

So often, when we get a revelation from God or take a step of spiritual growth, we think we're supposed to run right out and preach it to anyone who'll listen. We learn a few things from God, and then we start eyeing other people and feeling a little smug if they don't know what we know. We can hit people over the head with our spiritual wisdom.

But when the word of God comes to you, the last

thing it will make you is judgmental. When you understand from the Bible God's tremendous grace and mercy in sparing any of us from Satan's power, from death and hell, it will change you from a critic to a man or woman of prayer.

God wants you, like Ezra, to become an intercessor.

Now a lot of Christians stumble over that word *intercessor*. We know that Jesus is our great high Priest who lives forever to make intercession for us before the throne of God (see Heb. 4:14-16). He never accuses or judges us; He represents us in legal matters before God.

To be an intercessor simply means to be one who takes the place of another. Jesus died for us—when you and I were the condemned sinners. He made Himself sin on our behalf. He identified Himself with us completely.

That was what Ezra did. He put himself in the place of the people. He hadn't broken any law, but he said, "I am too ashamed to show my face to You, God, because we have disregarded Your commands."

Now when the people heard him praying in this way, an amazing thing happened. The people were cut in their hearts. They said, "No, Ezra, this isn't your fault." They confessed, "We have been unfaithful to our God" (Ezra 10:2).

Then, without any badgering or preaching from Ezra, they repented: "Let us make a covenant before our God to send away all these women....Let it be done according to the Law. Rise up [Ezra]; this matter is in your hands. We will support you, so take courage and do it" (vv. 3-4).

Revival fire had fallen! God's mission for Ezra was accomplished, and he didn't have to harangue anyone or preach a word. He could have said, in the words of Psalm 119:113, "I hate double-minded men," and he would have been perfectly right, according to the law.

But look at what was accomplished because Ezra understood grace and mercy, because he was humble and stood on the side of his people to plead with God for them.

God came and stood on the side of Ezra! Far from being stoned by the people, the quiet, bookish scribe became a public hero. He turned a terrible mess into a glorious, national spiritual revival.

The story of Ezra has some tremendous applications for us today.

The first principle, of course, is that we need to have an all- out commitment to the word of God. We need to meditate on it, to study it.

And we need to be in fellowship with others who not only say they believe it but base their lives upon it.

You see, today it's easy for a Christian to develop a so-called sophisticated attitude. On any given topic— like divorce, for instance—you hear so many Christians who say, "Well, I know what God's word says, but...." Or take the matter of godly authority in the home.

There are many Christian women who say, "Yes, I know the Bible says I'm to submit to my husband, but...." Likewise, there are men who know God tells them to love their wives, but....

Where do we get this attitude from? Why is it that we think we can question and dispute God's word?

Because we are listening to the voice of this age. It's a voice that tells us that God's word is really old-fashioned. That it spoke to people a long time ago, but it's not really for us today. After all, we're more intelligent than those old Hebrews. We know more about philosophy, psychology, the sciences. We are more sophisticated.

And so, even many Christians today are ashamed of the word of God. They don't want to appear out-of-step with their contemporaries, so they say, "I know what it says, but...."

Instead, like Ezra, we should be boldly saying, "I know the kind of sin everyone is into today, but I know what God's word says." And we should strive to find Christian friends who will not let us down in the faith but build us up. People who love God's word and live by it.

Now God doesn't want us to get off into exclusive little Christian cliques, where we think we're better than anyone else. He doesn't want us to stick our noses in the air and avoid others who aren't living according to His word. That's being judgmental.

No, God calls us as New Testament Christians to help

restore the brother or sister who has fallen. This is an important work of the church. Consider these instructions from Paul: "Brothers, if someone is caught in a sin, you who are spiritual should restore him gently" (Gal. 6:1).

You see, there is a spiritual way to restore people—gently. Without question, it involves prayer, the way Ezra prayed for the men of Israel.

One of the greatest spiritual ailments that can settle on any church—or on any individual—is a critical spirit. Once a critical attitude comes in, words become sharp and cutting, rather than a comfort that causes healing.

One of the most gentle, noble and patient Christians I think I've ever met has to be Evelyn (not her real name), a woman Wally and I met years ago.

One Sunday evening, at the end of a church service, Wally gave an altar call, offering to pray for salvation with anyone who needed to open his or her heart to Jesus. Evelyn and the woman sitting beside her immediately stood and came forward.

Wally asked, "Are you here to pray and receive Jesus as your Savior?"

Evelyn, who was teary-eyed, shook her head no. But the other woman said yes.

"Then you two are friends?" Wally asked.

"Well," said the one woman, nodding to Evelyn, "this is my husband's first wife."

It's amazing how a woman can read the veiled panic

135

in her husband's eyes when he shoots her a look that says, Come over here and help me—quick! Wally gave me one of those looks. Together we ministered to the woman who wanted prayer.

Later, from Evelyn, we heard an incredible story.

Evelyn's husband had been seeing this other woman secretly, and soon he left to marry her. At first, Evelyn was devastated. She was tempted to hate the woman and judge her because she'd taken Evelyn's husband away. After all, she had grounds to be angry because the Bible clearly says adultery is sin.

But every time she was tempted to pour out her anger to God, He seemed to remind her of the words of Jesus: "Anyone who hates his brother (or sister!) will be subject to judgment. Anyone who says, 'You fool,' will be in danger of the fire of hell" (see Matt. 5:22).

The Holy Spirit was nudging her to let go of the law and submit to His higher law of love!

So Evelyn made a supreme effort. She obeyed the word of God and began to pray for the new wife. She prayed to love her. She prayed for her salvation.

In doing so, two lives were changed for time and eternity: Evelyn escaped the bitterness that eats up so many men or women in her position. And, of course, her prayers brought "the other woman" to the Lord.

After that Sunday evening at church, we were in contact with Evelyn for quite some time. She continued to call the second wife, encouraging her to read her Bible and pray. She taught her about water baptism and got her into fellowship in a good church. She discipled this gal!

All through the word of God, and prayer.

Instead of allowing criticism and judgment to season your words with bitterness, become an Ezra. Like him, we need to pray, in the words of Psalm 119:

Teach me knowledge and good judgment (v. 66).
May your unfailing love be my comfort (v. 76).
May those who fear you turn to me (v. 79).
May my lips overflow with praise (v. 171).
May my tongue sing of your word! (v. 172).

At the outset of this chapter, we talked about that strange phenomenon: Just when we think everything's settled and at peace, new attacks and challenges pop up.

This applies to the word of God, too. Just when we think we've got deeper understanding and revelation, we need to be open to the Holy Spirit, who will show us how to apply it in any new situation we face.

You and I can know the word of God backwards and forwards—and it can be very hard and lifeless. But when we learn how to pray and mix God's word with the softening ointment of the Holy Spirit, it will bring healing and new life.

Without the Spirit of God praying and loving through us, we can sound like nothing more than a sounding gong or a clanging cymbal (see 1 Cor. 13:1).

But with the Holy Spirit, God's word in us can be the voice of revival. His ever-fresh application of the word will make us like fountains of water to the thirsty and streams of life to the dying.

You know, you can be dead right—but you're still dead. Isn't it a whole lot better to speak Spirit-born words that bring life? ✎

NINE

Deborah:
Just Do It!

One of Jesus' most powerful parables is the parable of the sower. It's so simple yet so rich in meanings!

The seed is the word of God: Some falls into hard hearts where it can't root. Some falls into shallow hearts that respond quickly but dry up when there's a little heat. More seed is scattered on thorny hearts concerned only with the cares of this world, and it's choked out. Then some falls into softened, well-tended hearts—and there's almost an explosion of life and abundance. I'll bet the disciples were in amazement at Jesus' explanation.

Jesus explained the different kinds of hearts we can have, but there was one important detail He didn't explain to His listeners: the seed.

You see, to the men and women of His day Jesus didn't have to explain the properties of a seed or what happens when you sow. Seed was something of a treasure to them. You couldn't send away for all the packets you wanted of any given variety from a mail-order catalog. You had to harvest the seeds carefully, store them where mice wouldn't get at them and sow them when conditions were just right—and, of course, calling attention to those conditions was Jesus' main purpose in telling the parable.

The people already knew the secret about seeds: Each one is a tough, little knot of power and life! Just give it anything like the right conditions, and it's practically unstoppable.

If you've ever sown grass seed, you'll know what I mean. If you do it on a windy day, you can have grass growing out of everywhere. You can be sowing it at one end of the yard, and the wind takes it—and it'll be trying to root and grow out of the dust on your blacktop driveway!

And that's the way it is with the word of God. If God's word has come to you in any scattered measure at all, it's at work in your heart.

You can feel it at work right now, can't you? Stop

for a moment and think about it.

Have you ever said something like this to yourself: Well, I know Jesus said you should love your enemies. I know He tells us to forgive, but—? Or, I know the Holy Spirit spoke to me and directed me to do such-and-such, but—?

So you have felt the seed-power of God's word trying to push through your heart!

I know that I have felt it. And sometimes I'm just as aware that I'm pushing back.

God's word always brings new life—and it brings change. And because we as human beings resist change, we can waste so much time, spend so much energy and miss so many blessings resisting the seed-power of God's word. God wants us to bear fruit, and we just act fruity!

We've already looked at so many beautiful and miraculous aspects of God's word. And you might still be thinking: I don't know, Marilyn. I've read the Bible for many years. I've heard so many sermons, listened to so many teaching tapes, not to mention radio and TV preachers. I've been to so many Bible studies. And I'm still having such a hard time as a Christian. Sometimes I feel as if I just haven't changed all that much, though I really *want* to change and grow as a Christian!

There's one little secret I've left till last. One key principle that will get you moving on with God. You can find it at work in the life of a neat woman I really admire.

141

The woman I'm referring to is Deborah.

Deborah lived in the time when judges ruled in Israel, and, in fact, Deborah was a judge. That fact, in itself, tells us something about the prevailing spirit of the day.

The book of Judges tells us it was a time when "everyone did as he saw fit" (Judg. 21:25). As the King James Version puts it, "Every man did that which was right in his own eyes." In other words, it was a lot like our own day when everyone wants to "do their own thing." Like men and women today, the folks of Deborah's day were very independent.

You see, Joshua's conquest of the land of Canaan took place in about 1450 B.C. He gained a lot of ground, but there were still heathen peoples, with filthy, idolatrous practices, left in the land. There were strong enemies left unconquered. At the time of Joshua's death, when the judges took over, the Israelites had not yet fully completed God's commandment to take every inch of ground and clean everyone else out.

In short, the people had gotten sidetracked. Each tribe had been given a portion of land. And within each tribe, the land was divided up among the clans and families. Every man (except the Levites, who were given cities of refuge to take care of) was given his own little plot of land.

I think they just got bogged down in the cares of their daily lives—farming, tending their herds—and, in their hearts, said: I've got business to tend to. I've got to take care of my own family and be a good steward of what God's blessed me with. I really don't have time to go out and fight these wars anymore. So what if some heathen practices are still mixed in around here? They won't hurt anything.

But neglecting God's commandments did hurt. Because the Israelites didn't get rid of the heathen influences, they developed a lazy, so-what attitude. Pretty soon, those influences started leading them away from God into idolatry. Over and over again, like a sad chorus, the writer of Judges says, "Once again, the Israelites did evil in the eyes of the Lord."

As a result, God had to allow the heathen people to oppress Israel—using them like a disciplinary rod on their spiritual hind parts! Then they'd shape up for a while—only to slide back into idolatry again. All because "each man did that which was right in his own eyes," rather than what the word of God had told him to do.

That's the way it had been during the lifetimes of three judges who came before Deborah.

When Deborah came onto the scene, the heathen king Jabin had been cruelly oppressing Israel for twenty years, and, for twenty years, the people had been crying out for help (see Judg. 4:3).

Now I want to ask you something. The first part of Judges tells about the brave exploits of three mighty and valiant men—Othniel, Ehud and Shamgar. But, in

Deborah's day, the people cried out to the Lord for deliverance for twenty years. Twenty years! I don't believe in getting down on the fellas, but where were the men all this time?

That was when the word of God came to Deborah, in a somewhat unusual way.

Deborah was a prophetess and the wife of Lappidoth. She held court beneath a palm tree in the hill country of Ephraim between Ramah and Bethel, which was north of Jerusalem. The Bible says she was "leading Israel at that time" (see Judg. 4:4), but she wasn't an out-front kind of leader.

The word of the Lord came to Deborah, and God let her know He was ready to free His people from the cruelty of Jabin. Jabin's commanding general, Sisera, had been riding roughshod over the Israelites—maybe even literally—with his nine hundred iron chariots.

The Lord told Deborah to call in Barak and send him out as a general to lead the people. Listen to this inspiring word from the Lord to Barak: "The Lord, the God of Israel, commands you: 'Go, take with you ten thousand men of Naphtali and Zebulun and lead the way to Mount Tabor. I will lure Sisera...to the Kishon River and give him into your hands' " (Judg. 4:6-7).

God gave Barak the command, the people who were to help him, the plan and the place, and the promise of victory. But Barak still waffled. He said to Deborah, "If you go with me, I will go; but if you don't go with me, I won't go" (v. 8).

You might shake your head at Barak's weak-spined character. You might say, boy, with that kind of assurance from God, victory was his for the taking—like picking an apple off a tree. And it's true. Even Deborah said to him, "Because of the way you are going about this, the honor will not be yours, for the Lord will hand Sisera over to a woman" (v. 9).

But I want you to look at a subtler thing that's going on here.

In essence, Barak bounced the ball back into Deborah's court. In his mind's eye, he was seeing those nine hundred iron chariots and thinking how it would feel to have their wheels dice him up like an onion. He was thinking of spears and arrows flying, swords slashing and the blood of men soaking the ground. And Deborah was expecting him to go out there on just a word!

So when he replied to Deborah he was really saying, "You seem pretty confident and self-assured sitting here under this shady palm tree. It's pretty easy for you to tell me that God has commanded *me* to go out into battle. But if you really believe this word from the Lord is true, then put your money where your mouth is. Let's see if you trust that word enough to come out into the thick of it!"

Maybe you've caught yourself giving advice to someone—assuring someone of a certain principle in God's word—and then a little voice inside your head says, "How about you? Do you believe God's word enough to put your full weight on it?" It's easy to pass out instructions on how to fight a war to someone who's headed for the front lines, especially when you're sitting at home in comfort and safety. But God doesn't want us to be armchair generals.

One of God's most life-changing words came to Deborah through Barak. I believe He spoke deeply to her heart when Barak said, "How about you, Deborah? Do you believe what you say you believe—enough to go out there and stake your life on it?"

At that moment, I think, Deborah had to face a choice. She could have said, "Where are all the big, heroic men? Let's call in someone else to do it, Lord." She could have complained—but she seemed to know in her heart that God was working on her, too.

Deborah did go out to battle with Barak and the ten thousand Israelites. She was there when God sent rain so that Sisera's iron chariot sank in the mud, and he had to escape on foot. She was probably among the first to hear the news that Sisera had hidden in the tent of Heber, a Kenite, and that Heber's wife, Jael, had driven a tent-peg through his head while he slept in her tent. (Incidentally, if you're wondering how a woman could do such a bloody thing, you need to know something about ancient Mideast culture. Sisera had gone in to sleep in Heber's inner tent, which was where women slept. In the Arab culture, the only person allowed in that intimate place was a woman's husband. If her husband found another man in there, she could be put to death. So Jael killed Sisera out of self-defense!)

I believe Deborah recognized God's word to her: It's time to stop saying you trust in My word, and time to start putting your faith into action.

There are lots of other points we could make from the life of Deborah. But I want to focus on one point only: When God's word came to her, she put her weight down on it. She said, "If God's word is true, I can put my faith in it, and He will never let me fall."

Yes, God carried her through the battle so that she saw victory—but she had to get into Barak's chariot and ride!

That is the key that some of us are missing. God speaks to us all the time—through the word, through speakers and teachers, through counsel from Christian friends. But do we apply it? Do we put the full weight of our lives down on it? Do we act on it, so that it becomes real and powerful and living and as active as a two-edged sword?

If you get nothing else from this book, get this: You can say you're a "New Testament, born-again" Christian and still act as if you're stuck in the Old Testament when everyone did not have the light of the Holy Spirit, not to mention His comfort and the assurance of His presence and power every day.

But we have that assurance! We have great and precious promises that are "yes and amen" through Christ (see 2 Cor. 1:20).

Hagar was driven into the wilderness in despair and hopelessness. But the apostle Peter assures us that God has "given us a new birth into a living hope" (1 Pet. 1:3).

Esther suffered through a fiery trial in the dark oppression of Persia to purify her spirit for God's use. But John promises us that if we simply turn to God and confess our sins and impurities, the blood of Jesus will "purify us from all unrighteousness" (1 John 1:9).

Eli's spiritual insight became dimmed; he grew fat, and his sons died because he gave into his flesh. But Paul promises that we can "live by faith and not by sight" (2 Cor. 5:7).

Mighty Elijah suffered burnout because, even though he had God's plan, he tried to fight God's battles in his own way. But Paul gives us the insight that we can be "transformed into [Christ's] likeness with ever-increasing glory, which comes from the Lord, who is the Spirit" (2 Cor. 3:18). We don't have to flame out briefly and then fizzle. We can "shine like stars in the universe" and finish the race God calls us to so we won't be ashamed to stand before Him (Phil. 2:14-16).

Like Habakkuk, we can stop blaming, resisting and grumbling against God. Like Paul, the great apostle to us Gentiles, we can learn that our weakness is no problem for God. We can draw from the deep wells of His grace and know that, even in dark times, His grace will flood us with overcoming power that's more than "sufficient" (2 Cor. 12:9).

With the simple faith of Ruth, you and I can also enter into God's great plan of salvation. No matter who you are, where you came from—no matter what your past sins or present flaws—God wants to use you. As Matthew reported at the end of his Gospel: All authority has been given to you in heaven and on earth. Go and make disciples of every nation (see Matt. 28:18-19).

And like Ezra, you can stop putting yourself down, telling yourself that God can't use you because you're no hero. We know from Paul that, "The eye cannot say to the hand, 'I don't need you.'...On the contrary, those parts of the body that seem to be weaker are indispensable" (1 Cor. 12:21-22).

Finally, like Deborah, we can face Satan's worst attacks. Like Luke, we have heard the word that comes from the Captain of our faith, Jesus. For He declared, "I saw Satan fall like lightning" (Luke 10:18).

Yes, we know all these great truths from the Bible, and only one thing remains. We can step out into faith and win.

For as Jesus said, "Now that you know these things, you will be blessed if you do them" (John 13:17).

In every area of your life, God's word can bring change—life, peace, provision, freedom from struggle, victory over Satan and evil circumstances—but you must throw yourself into the battle. God not only wants to change events; He wants to transform you.

It's this transforming process that will slowly—day by day, battle by battle—change you.

Embrace it! Love it. Trust it. Ask God to show you how to apply the word to your life by the power of the Holy Spirit. Then you can have the joy of knowing that, when you stand before Him, He'll smile at you like a proud father whose child obeys his every last word.

And you'll have the assurance that His first words to you—on the day you meet Him face-to-face and all your mistakes are wiped out for good—will be these: "Well done! C'mon in. I've had some great rewards planned for you all along!"